T0265850

This is an exclusive signed edition of

WHO'S
THAT
GIRL?

EVE

WHO'S
THAT
GIRL?

WHO'S THAT GIRL?

A MEMOIR

EVE

WITH KATHY IANDOLI

HANOVER
SQUARE
PRESS

HANOVER
SQUARE
PRESS™

ISBN-13: 978-1-335-99470-7

Who's That Girl? Signed Exclusive Edition

Hanover Square Press
22 Adelaide St. West, 41st Floor
Toronto, Ontario M5H 4E3, Canada
HanoverSqPress.com

Printed in U.S.A.

Dedicated to My Family: Past, Present, Future.

WHO'S
THAT
GIRL?

PREFACE

THE GIFT AND THE CURSE

When I was little, I was *convinced* that I was cursed with the name "Eve." Who could blame me, really? My grandma was a Jehovah's Witness, and she would bring me to the Kingdom Hall for worship, where all I ever heard about was how bad Eve was. Nobody liked her ass. She's literally described in the Bible and other holy books as the reason why there is evil in this world. I mean, Eve made Adam bite the apple even though he gave her his rib... You know the story. It doesn't matter your religion or your faith, everybody figures that Eve was bad news. So to be *named* Eve? Imagine carrying that around in your head all day. Thinking you're named after the woman who invented original sin? Ugh.

I wanted answers. I'd ask my mom all the time why she named me that, and eventually she told me that I "just looked like one." Wow, okay. My middle name is "Jihan"— an alternate spelling of "Jahan"—because my mother liked the name "Shah Jahan," who was the Mughal emperor of India who built the Taj Mahal. At least I had that going for me. So my name is Eve Jihan, and honestly, there really is much more to my name, but I didn't learn just how important it all was until I was much older.

The name "Eve" actually means "the first woman" or "the first lady" in the Bible, and "Jihan" is Persian for "the world" or "the universe." So technically, my name means "the First Woman of the Universe." When I really understood what that meant—I mean, when it *really* clicked for me—you couldn't tell me shit after that. I knew I was put here for a reason, and I channeled all of that gumption into adopting this "by any means necessary" attitude in the game, where I was gonna get things done regardless. My mother used to tell me that as a kid, if someone told me "no" or that I couldn't do something, I would go ahead and do it anyway. So subconsciously, I always embodied that name without realizing it. I was never the type to be told that I "can't"—no matter what it was—because in my mind I always could regardless. It's also the main reason why I never competed with anyone. If I knew I had a specific purpose on this planet and knew what my name meant, then how would I look sizing myself up next to someone else? I've just never really cared about competition with other people. Okay, except for maybe *one*.

September 14, 1999, was the date that my debut album hit the streets. *Let There Be Eve… Ruff Ryders' First Lady*—the title alone showed the world I was, in fact, Eve, the First Woman of the Ruff Ryders universe. It was a moment that I had waited for my whole life, and the culmination of everything I had worked toward. On the day my album was released, I found out that Jay-Z had called and wanted to talk to me, and it was like an added layer of excitement. A few years ago, there was this question that was posed on social media about whether you'd take $500,000 or have a meet-ing with Jay-Z. When Jay-Z called me in '99, I technically had both. I mean, he'd only been active in the music in-dustry for a few years at that time, but his name rang bells. So it meant something to get a phone call from Jay-Z. I ex-pected a congratulations from him, and I got it. Well, *sort of.*

He did open the call with "Congratulations," but then he chased it with something like…but don't be too upset, because female hip-hop albums don't really do that well. Huh? Now, let's be clear: in 1999, *no one* was doing as good as they could have been doing in hip-hop, or any other genre, because Napster had just come out that summer. The whole game was on high alert, and everybody was throwing around terms like "music piracy" or, as we liked to call it in hip-hop, "bootlegging." But for Jay-Z to call me up and explain to me how the odds were stacked against me as a *woman* when *everyone* was fighting an uphill battle was ballsy.

So I had to show him.

To me, it felt more like a challenge than an insult. A bat-tery was immediately put in my back. In that moment, it felt like another (male) roadblock on my ride to fame. Before my album even touched record store shelves, I had already been through that major label rinse cycle of being signed, unsigned, then signed again—all at the hands of men who loved my lyrical talent, yet if I opened my mouth to voice anything but a bar, I was a problem.

My debut album went to number one on the Billboard 200, making me the third female rapper in history to achieve that feat. It went double platinum, which, again, in '99 was hard for anyone to do—but I did it. Take *that*, Napster! Take *that*, Jay-Z! So yeah, I channeled my am-bitions and frustrations into "competing" with Jay, or at least Jay's perception of the success of women in hip-hop.

And you may find that ironic, but I needed someone that I had to consistently prove wrong. Some might laugh that I chose him. I doubt he would stare at himself in the mirror and ask, "What Would Eve Do?" I get it.

Look, we all have our own Invisible Bully, the person we battle in our minds, so to speak. Sometimes it's your coworker always giving you backhanded compliments about your performance in the company—celebrating your wins, yet always making sure to add a caveat. And in many ways, Jay-Z was that coworker and hip-hop was our company. So my innate response was to tip over the proverbial water cooler and flip some desks on the way to the corner office. Jay and I have always been cool, and I'm sure he never even knew what that call did for my drive. Now he does, and I guess I should thank him for it.

The reality, though, is he was just a representation of the *real* bully, for me and so many other women: the music industry. Our success stories are always undersold. Even when we're lapping men, we're still called "slept on" or "underrated" as a means of keeping us below the industry sea level. For me, it was simultaneously being called the pit bull in a skirt *and* the underdog. My moves were drowning out those words, but they were still used to keep me down. I'm speaking both for myself and other women here, especially Black women. Telling me that I was going to fail wasn't protecting my fragile female heart from disappointment; it was perpetuating a cycle that I wanted to break. Did I do that? Many times. Sometimes I won; sometimes I lost. But eventually I realized that if the music industry wasn't going to let me be the first woman of their universe, then I had no choice.

I had to leave and go build my own.

1

MURDER STREET

THREE

When you look at a map of Philadelphia, it almost re-sembles the shape of a hand making the "peace" sign. I guess it's only right that it's called the City of Brotherly Love, though sometimes that nickname is a little ironic if you ask me. Philly was my home, though, and no matter where I've gone since then, it still is.

I was born on November 10, 1978, at Penn Presbyterian Hospital in West Philadelphia. My mother, Julie, was sev-enteen when she had me and named me Eve Jihan Jeffers. My father, Jerry, was around the same age and played bass in a band. That's how my parents first met. He also used to deejay in my grandmom's basement during the summer. He'd fill that basement with people, and as a little kid I'd go there to watch him spin soul records.

For the first part of my childhood, my mom's family and I all lived in one apartment in the high-rises of the Mill Creek

Housing Project in West Philly. You wanna talk about a full house? It was me, my mom, my grandmom, my granddad, my aunt Karen, my uncle Johnny, and eventually my cousin Takeya (I was six when she was born). We were packed into a four-bedroom place, where I shared a bedroom with my mom. Aunt Karen and Takeya shared a room, my grandparents had theirs, and then my uncle Johnny had his own. So basically, my whole family lived under one roof. I do have two other uncles—my uncle Jimmy and my uncle Jeffrey. Uncle Jimmy was in and out of prison for a lot of my life; Uncle Jeffrey wasn't allowed around the house when my granddad was home. I never asked any questions about that.

As a little kid, it felt like West Philly was just a whole lot of big buildings on top of other big buildings, including my own at Mill Creek. The story of Mill Creek goes that the three high-rise buildings in our projects, and all of the surrounding low-rises, were built on top of this one creek—Mill Creek—so the land was never actually steady enough to hold anything up. The foundation could literally cave in at any moment, and the residents just had to live with that hanging over their heads every single day. So on top of all the other fears you could have while living in West Philadelphia, I could add being swallowed by the earth to my list. Mill Creek eventually became famous again in 2000 for something called the Lex Street Massacre, when four guys shot ten people in a crack house on Lex Street over a busted-up car and some drug money. Seven of them died and three were injured. It made history as the deadliest mass murder in all of Philadelphia. That was right around where I grew up. Now everything is knocked down, and they planted a sustainable community farm there. The creek is still sitting right under it.

After my cousin Takeya was born, we all moved down to the low-rise houses on a little side street called Olive Walk. The narrow little street had all these redbrick box houses, and each shared a wall and a stoop with the house next to it. We had a little grass—I wouldn't call it a park or anything, but it was enough to play on, and you could see one of the high-rise buildings right in front of us, along with a big-ass empty field across the street where nothing was ever built. If you walked through the alleyways and over to the high-rises, you'd reach the main road, named Meredith Street, but everyone knew it as Murder Street. That nickname needs no explanation. The streets of West Philadelphia were checkered with guns and crack, and the unfortunate victims were the people who lived along those streets—some dying from violence, others from overdoses. Pick your poison. I never really understood that aspect of Philly until I was a little older. I just knew it was this big city to me, one that I would spend most of my time staring at through the train windows on the El.

At home, I always felt like my surroundings were so dark. It's hard to explain. We would go to our neighbors' house sometimes and their home just felt so much lighter. It wasn't like we had darker wallpaper or paint on the walls, but even as a kid I just felt a darker aura in my home. My granddad had gradually developed a drinking problem, so sometimes he would come home drunk at night, turn on all the lights in the house and just start yelling and arguing with everyone. We walked on eggshells whenever he was around, and every time he came home from work, we'd all run upstairs and hide. Then one day, many years later, he just changed and became this smiling, lighthearted person. It was crazy, but a welcome switch. He stopped drinking, but I can't just credit it to that. In my adult years, dealing with my own relationship with alcohol, I learned to acknowledge that "come to Jesus" moment, because it was a total energetic shift that I noticed in him (and later me). He wasn't very affectionate for most of my life, though; like the first time he hugged me was in my thirties, and I was freaked out. My grandmom is a Jehovah's Witness, which is how I wound up at the Kingdom Hall. She's still devout too, waiting for those 144,000 to be saved or go to heaven. My grandparents were always a mystery to me, even though my entire childhood was spent living with them. My cousin Takeya and I used to joke and say they must've been like Bonnie and Clyde on the run and moved to Philly to set up a new life. Their backstory was like a total secret. All I knew was that my granddad was from Alabama and was in the military, and my grandmom was from Ohio and had a sister who she used to write to. And that's all I really know about them to this day. Since my grandmom was a Jehovah's Witness, we didn't celebrate Christmas in our home—or any birthdays—but I would watch *The Sound of Music* and *The Nutcracker* when they aired during the holidays, and that was my own little Christmas. My mom still bought me gifts though, and since my aunt Karen loved the holidays, she'd celebrate with us outside of the house.

On my father's side, the whole family is from North Carolina, so I spent my summers there from age six until I was about twelve. My grandparents—his parents—lived up the street from me in Philly, so I could literally walk up the hill to their house to visit them and spend time with my dad. Eventually, though, he stopped showing up. But I still did. And as much as I loved my grandparents and my cousins, they weren't the ones I wanted to be with. I wanted to be with my dad. He admitted to me years later that he had a drug problem, and that's why he kept away from me, which I respected. And he never tried to show up once I became famous like, "Daddy's home!" I respected that too. But as a kid who just wanted to hang out with her dad, I didn't know what was going on when he started vanishing back then. So I matched his energy, and one day I said, "I'm done," and stopped going to visit him at my grandparents' house. I couldn't take it anymore and had to tell myself "I'm good." He just kept disappointing me, not showing up when I invited him to my school graduations or anything else. When my mom and I moved farther away, it got easier for me to space out the visits too. I held on to that anger, though, and I wasn't afraid to show him whenever I did see him. He and his brothers used to call me "Evil Eve" because I was always pouting when I was around them. I never smiled and always had an attitude. As an adult, I realize it was just me trying to get a response out of my dad. Something. I also realized that same anger fueled my desire and need to be seen and heard throughout most of my early adult life. I channeled *all* of that rage when I first picked up a microphone. But as a kid? I just wanted my dad's attention—though honestly I *always* wanted *everyone's* attention.

When you're living in a packed house with all adults (and one bassinet holding your baby cousin) it's not easy to get the attention you're seeking. So my little dramatic ass would find any corner of the house where everyone was within earshot, and I'd sit down and sing a little song I'd made up: "Nooooobody loves me. Nooooobody cares." Did I really believe that? Of course not, but I figured I could Jedi mind trick them into playing with me or hearing all about my day if I convinced them that I felt unloved. When it didn't work, I'd get even more annoyed. I just had so much energy, and I wanted everyone in on watching me use it. My mom used to tell me that I should've been born a boy with the way I acted. I loved to wrestle with the other kids in my neighborhood, and when we did, then I *had* to be Hulk Hogan—or the Undertaker. I'd take either, but I had to be one or the other. I also wanted to play sports, like softball—and I loved being scared by horror movies. That was all my aunt Karen's fault. My mom was in school and worked a lot, so I spent a lot of time with Aunt Karen. She took me to see all the movies I wasn't supposed to, like *A Nightmare on Elm Street.* My mom used to say to her, "Why do you keep taking her to see this shit?" because I'd get so scared, but I loved it. It's why horror is still my favorite film genre to this day. My aunt Karen was always more like a big sister to me than an auntie. We were only nine years apart, while me and my cousin Takeya were six years apart. Being an only child for most of my childhood, it really felt like I had a big sister and a little sister in them. Plus, my aunt Karen put me onto hip-hop. She loved music so much, so all day, every day, music was around me. She even slept with the radio on. I'd hear LL Cool J coming from her room, and I'd run in there to listen. I had this deep love of music and the arts that I just couldn't explain at that age, but I knew I needed it around me. I was also obsessed with words. I started writing poems when I was in elementary school at Alain Locke. I even won a bunch of awards. If "RAP" stands for "rhythm and poetry," I had the "poetry" part down pretty fast.

I didn't know exactly what to do with the "rhythm" part, though, but as a kid I just wanted to somehow be a part of the music. At first, I wanted to take piano lessons, but we didn't really have the money for all of that. Reality hit when my mom took me to a place for lessons across the street from my elementary school and a requirement was having a piano in your home, and we definitely didn't have one of those. After that, I told myself that one day, when I grew up, I was going to have a piano in my house. In school, I wanted to play the cello, but they told me I wasn't big enough, so instead I had to play the violin. I was so mad. They gave the cello to this other chick, so I learned how to play "Baa, Baa, Black Sheep" on the violin and then quit. I also sang in the school choir, and after begging my mom, she let me take ballet and tap lessons. I just wanted to be close to the music, whether I was singing or dancing or picking up and then ditching an instrument.

By the time I was twelve, the whole family picked up again and moved over to Wyalusing Avenue. You could say we got out of the hood, but it was still kind of hood over there too. I transferred over to Our Lady of Victory School for my last two years of elementary school. That's where I started really getting into my own musical tastes. My mom bought me a Discman and I was able to pick out two CDs, so I got Nirvana's *Nevermind* and Bob Marley's *Legend*. I was already into reggae and dancehall with my Buju Banton cassettes and whatnot, so I figured I'd add a Bob Marley CD to my collection too. By that point, my mom had been dating her boyfriend Ron for a few years, and he took me and my friend Yvette to our first concert, Shabba Ranks, when I was twelve. We wore matching dashikis and had these thick-ass braids like Patra did in her "Queen of the Pack" video. Once I saw the music live right in front of me onstage, I knew I wanted to be up there too. I had been singing in the choir for years at this point, but I figured that wasn't going to get me enough attention since all the other girls sang too.

So I decided to rap.

Yvette and I linked up with two other girls at school to form our own little group called DGP, which stood for "Dope Girl Posse." We were just starting out, covering songs by Another Bad Creation and Color Me Badd, you know, all the hot shit at the time. Our touring circuit was only the school talent shows (and sometimes block parties) but we made it work, and I just started taking it *real* seriously. Like, even though I was a kid, something in me knew that this was going to be the building blocks to *something*, so I couldn't half step. But DGP hit a major snag when my mom and Ron decided to get married and find a place of their own. So now I had a stepdad, and before I knew it we were moving off Wyalusing Ave and into the suburbs of Germantown as our own little family. I still got to hang out with my aunt Karen and grandparents every weekend, but Germantown was like twenty minutes away from West Philly, which in kid math might as well have been three hours away. DGP couldn't survive that commute, so we kind of fizzled out and I became a little solo artist. Within a year, my brother Farrod was born, and I started my freshman year at Martin Luther King High School.

Now, I know in most cities around the world, anything named after Martin Luther King is pretty terrible (sadly), but my high school was extra terrible. There was a lot of unnecessary shit going on in there; it was just wild. We had a police station right there *in* the high school—that's how bad it was! Our principal tried to be like Joe Clark in *Lean on Me* and walked around carrying a baseball bat, and we were all like, "Wait, are you smoking crack?"

In the midst of that chaos, I temporarily found peace in Islam. It wasn't too far off for me to be interested in becoming a Muslim, since my stepdad was in the Nation of Islam and Philly is full of Muslim people from all walks of life. I made this new friend who was Muslim and she wore the hijab, and she was also really cool and outspoken. I processed that as, "Hey, you can be cool and covered too!" It's true, but with me, I just have to go *all*-in. Like immediately. I'm talking about full-fledged Sunni Muslim after that. I wore a hijab, started going by the name "Mecca," and learned every surah and hadith that I could fit into my newly teenage brain. Like, I could recite the first surah of the Quran—the Al-Fatiha—frontwards and backwards. There was even a place in school where we could pray during the day. The part that I missed in the brochure, though, is that you shouldn't really curse and you can't smoke weed, and I definitely wanted in on both of those. Plus, I was getting more drawn to rapping, and to me it felt like that was a conflict of interest. I didn't wanna come across as a hypocrite. So after about five months, I took off my hijab and said my final Bismillah.

After that, I guess you could say I converted to the Zulu Nation of Hip-Hop. I continued writing poems, which evolved into writing full-fledged rhymes. That's when something really came alive in me, like I was plugged in. It's hard to explain that moment when it all made sense— when my poems and the music from Aunt Karen's bedroom, and my dad's soul records, and my love of rap and reggae, and even playing my cello, piano and violin just all started swirling into my developing mind and something entirely new came out. It was something beautiful to me, and something I needed to get out and share with the world. After that, I needed a place other than my note-book to put those words, because I couldn't just keep them to myself any longer. I had to show them off.

So I found the best place in the world to showcase them: the cypher.

2

NOT YOUR AVERAGE JAWN

In Philly slang, the word *jawn* could literally refer to *any* noun—a person, a place, or a thing. So you can say something like, "Did you see that jawn the other day?" or "Pass me that jawn real quick," or "You headin' to that jawn tomorrow night?" The word has many functions, and it's as signature to Philly as a cheesesteak. It's so popular that it's even been added to Dictionary.com. True story. And you can have just one jawn or multiple jawns. Usually, though, when you're talking about a human jawn, it's in reference to a girl.

Well...this jawn couldn't run. At least not as fast as the cops in my high school. They were always chasing me for one reason or another. I had to be the most irresponsible responsible teenager. At home, my mom had to go back to work, so I had to be the one to take care of my little brother when my mom and stepdad were working. Farrod was *my* baby in my head, especially since I'd begged my mother to have him. So when she did, he was mine after that. In the mornings, I'd bring him to day care, and then after school I would pick him up and watch him until my mom came home. And yeah, I guess that gave me *some* responsibility, since part-time, I was in charge of keeping a child alive, but I still managed to find new and creative ways to fuck up and get in trouble. For one, I felt like MLK wasn't the school I was supposed to be in. I wanted to go to the Philadelphia High School for the Creative and Performing Arts. That's the school where Boyz II Men met, and where I felt I belonged. I didn't even know if I had to audition to get in; I just knew I had to be there. My mother didn't agree. She didn't think an arts-based school was going to give me the most well-rounded education. Little did she know that MLK was *not* it. I had to make sure I rebelled whenever I could.

If I wasn't going to be in a school that focused on the arts, then I didn't want to go to class at all. Like ever. I was really good at basketball, and I even won some trophies and plaques when I played. And I was very smart, but once I decided that I wanted to rap, it almost felt like school was an afterthought. Don't you go to school to figure out your life? Mine was figured out! I was rapping. So really, I didn't need to be there. I wanted to be smoking weed and writing rhymes. Class was getting in the way of that, so I kept trying to cut, which led to those regularly scheduled sprint sessions with the cops posted up in our high school police station. They used to call me "Turtle," because I never ran fast enough and would always get caught. The cops would be like, "Just...stop running. We're going to catch you, you know." How embarrassing—even though I did fool them enough to cut class regularly. But what I lacked in speed, I made up for in the rap cyphers.

Stepping into the cypher as a girl is a whole other experience. You're not just there to battle the dudes; it's like you're carrying your entire gender on your back when you show up. Typically everyone stands around in a circle; sometimes you're there to diss everybody, while other times you're there to just impress everybody. For me, I always showed up to accomplish both.

So that was the setup: a bunch of dudes standing around in a circle talking shit to each other. Plus me.

And sure, I was cute—still a tomboy, even though I liked looking pretty—but I was a menace. And the last thing I wanted was to show up to a battle, pretty face and boobs first. I had to make sure my rhymes were *sharp*, but also men are basic and it's easy to insult them. Preparing to verbally fight them was easy to me, though I still had to be ready with rhymes up my sleeve. You could call it my Scorpio self-awareness, but I've never been the best freestyler. I'll be the first to admit that. Having a background in poetry, anything I put out there had to be a little organized or else I would fly off the rails. The same approach applied to my rap writing. So every battle I was in, I made sure to have my framework down: I'd talk about their dick size (always small, no matter what), their inability to get girls (especially not me), and how weak their rhymes were (goes without saying). Everything else would just fall into place, and I was well equipped for some on-the-spot madness.

I also had to fuck you up in English *and* Patois...

See, there was this big war in my high school between the Americans and the Jamaicans, where we would have these crazy stampedes inside of the school. They would start as something small and then erupt into these huge, knock-down, drag-out fights. People would be pulling down fire alarms when a big fight broke out, and then we'd have to race down the hallway with alarms blaring and run out of the school or else we'd be pepper sprayed by the high school cops conveniently posted up there. They damn sure didn't call me Turtle then, because the adrenaline rush to avoid pepper spray totally took over me. Cutting class on those days wasn't hard; once the chaos ensued I would just keep running right off the school grounds. On the lighter side of that American/Jamaican war, though, were the rap battles. Naturally, I needed to be a part of them whenever the opportunity presented itself. So I was doing double duty, battling whoever wanted it. Since I loved Jamaican culture and had a lot of Jamaican friends, it was nothing to learn a little Patois to sprinkle into the battles.

Yeah, I was Jafakin' it.

I linked up with another girl and we were trying to work on some music things for a while, but I think deep down I knew that I wanted to stand on my own. I also hated waiting for anyone else to get me off the ground. I can be impatient that way, because once I really knew this was my dream, it was like now or never and I just had to hurry it all along. I started hanging around a local studio in Center City, where I met this kid named Scott Storch. He was a skinny kid playing the piano in oversized clothes (so basically he's always looked the exact same way). Scott was only a few years older than me, but he was already producing for the Roots. Everybody knew who Scott was, and everybody knew who the Roots were. I was a *huge* Roots fan, especially Black Thought. To me, he was the archetype of an emcee and felt like the pride of our city. I was going to Roots concerts when I was like fourteen years old, completely in awe of Black Thought. I loved MC Lyte and I loved Queen Latifah, but I'd be lying if I said that when I picked up the mic, I didn't have Black Thought at the front of my mind.

In the early '90s, Philadelphia was like the cool cousin of New York City. Will Smith had already put West Philadelphia on the map with *The Fresh Prince of Bel-Air*, so we had that to hold on to, along with the Roots, who back then had their first album out and were throwing these big house parties where all of the local talent came to perform. Anytime I saw Black Thought, I'd act like a total goofball. Most of the girls did. He didn't pay any of us any mind; he was focused on blowing up. I totally knew the feeling. Seeing the Roots do it, though? That was all the inspiration I needed, because when your "neighbors" are out there making it happen, that means you have a shot. I held on tightly to that.

While I was hanging out in the studio, watching other artists record at their sessions, it only added to that motivation for me. When you see the music being made, you're aware that it's actually happening. It's tangible. The excitement of watching the magic unfold firsthand was intoxicating, but I also knew that it was within my reach. I wasn't cocky, but I was confident. I was completely certain that I was going to be the one in the studio cutting my own album one day. One day very soon.

There was this older kid named Marv who lived around the corner from my high school, who I regard as my *first* producer, because he was the one I was really actively working with 24/7 back then. I would show up to school in the morning and maybe go to first and second period, and then I would kind of declare the school day done and cut the rest of my classes. That is, if Turtle didn't get caught. If I did, then I'd just wait a little longer to dip for the day. I only had a specific amount of time to get my music in before my big-sister responsibilities kicked in. That time to make music (and smoke weed) was precious, because it was limited, so the sooner I got to my producer's house, the better. Once I did, we'd just be smoking weed in his basement and I'd be writing songs. Even though Marv made beats too, my favorite thing to do was listen to some of my favorite in-strumentals, smoke weed, and write some verses over them. Whether it was a Mobb Deep or a Lil' Kim beat, I loved writing "my versions" of the songs. I also started selling weed to finance this mission of mine, along with working at Gilly Jeans on South Street. I had to stack as much money as I could. That independent artist life is pretty broke when you're not being paid to do it yet. It's even worse as a teen-ager, since you're literally starting from nothing. And I'm not just talking about being able to afford to look nice; I'm talking about wanting to have money for anything at all, like getting from one place to the next. You couldn't walk everywhere, even if you tried, and only a few people had cars. There were a lot of obstacles, the kind that feel enor-mous when you're that young.

I was no stranger to local talent shows by then, but that was just a place to practice in between open mics and other stuff out in Philly. I really started going in, to the point where I knew it wasn't just me thinking I could do it. Com-plete strangers started believing in me. I felt like if I was racking up all of these successful shows and people were loving me, and I was killing it in the cyphers and getting all of these great responses, then that must mean some-thing. To me, though, it just felt like it wasn't happening

fast enough, so I kept trying to hurry it along. I was looking for a manager to help me level up more quickly. It all
just felt like suspended animation. Here I was at like fifteen years old, already annoyed that I wasn't a rap superstar.

A year prior, I sat my mother down on my bed and let her
know that her daughter was going to be a full-time rapper,
and that I wasn't going to college. I did bargain with her
that I would finish high school, one way or another. I told
her, "Mom, I know you probably want me going to college, but this is going to be my life. I really want to do this."
I was dead serious—again, at fifteen. She was surprisingly
supportive, and said, "If this is what you really want to do
and you're not hurting anyone, then do it." I shouldn't have
been shocked, because my mom has always been so accepting of people and meeting them exactly where they are in
their lives. My friends even called her "Mom" and would
call her for advice. Even though she was strict with me, she
let me express myself to the fullest—whether it was getting
my nose pierced at twelve, or later cutting off all my hair and
bleaching it. My mom always let me be me, so why would
this situation be an exception? I had this preconceived notion, though, of what college specifically meant to my mom,
especially since she became a young mother and had to hold
off on college for herself. She eventually worked at Wendy's
and went to business school at night to get her corporate
job. So I was carrying a whole other bag of thoughts in my
head. Still, I knew I could make it if I tried. Determina-
tion was in my genes, after all, and watching other people
make it meant that I had to. I had no choice, in my mind.
It was a lot of pressure to put on myself, but that was only
the start. I also told myself that if I didn't make it in a year
(meaning, when I was seventeen), then I was done and I

would quit. I had a backup plan to attend New York University and major in Special Effects Makeup. So basically I threatened *myself* with going to college. It wasn't the most helpful pep talk, but it was the only one I could think of at that moment in my life. Surely a self-imposed ultimatum would get me where I needed to be in no time.

Obviously, that wasn't the case.

But to me, there was just no way that I could ever keep going with just a dream and no reality. All of the props were fine, but I wasn't seeing the results. Mainly, though, I needed money—and I needed it fast. There was only one thing left to do: Eve had to take a bite out of the Big Apple.

3

THE LAZIEST STRIPPER AT THE CLUB

I'm standing topless in front of some middle-aged man, smiling with his legs spread, like he's ready for me to hop on and start grinding on him. I'm already over it, but I sit down and swing my legs around him...reluctantly. He whispers some dumb shit into my ear about what he'd love to do to me, his voice all hot and breathy. I roll my eyes and crack a tiny smile. I whisper back with a proposition, but not the one he's expecting. "Let me rap for you," I say to him. "And if you don't like it, then you get a free lap dance." He accepts. Who wouldn't? You can't beat that, right? As far as I was concerned, any one of these men at the strip club were a part of my audience, and one way or another I was going to be heard.

And paid.

A few moments later, I hop off that potential hell ride triumphantly, knowing that I just rapped for this man with my boobs out. *And* he's still tipping me when I didn't even give him a lap dance. He could've had his night made if he didn't like my bars, but he did. They all did. They always do. Tonight I'm Destiny; last week I was Raven. "You can't keep changing your name!" my boss at the Golden Lady yelled at me. I was getting on his last nerve. "Your clients need to recognize you by just one name so they can ask for you when they come in!" I didn't listen to his ass. I'd be Desire next week, Midnight, Fantasy, Felicia, Frankfurt. I don't care. One name would make me an employee, which would make this a career. And it wasn't. I was just acting… in a temporary role.

The dancing industry is pretty sobering. I'm no expert *at all*, since my dancing days began and ended within the span of two months, but everything I experienced made me feel guilty. And depressed. I knew I didn't *have* to be there, and I'm not saying that dismissively. Some girls were there to feed their families; they had kids to take care of and a roof over their head to pay for. I had a mom and a stepdad who weren't pressuring me to do anything but maybe further my education after graduating high school. I was seventeen, and I could be home with a normal-ass job. But in my mind, things at home with my family weren't really going that well. My brother Farrod was growing up, so he was no longer just a little baby but becoming a whole little human. To me, the house was getting too crowded. Add to that, I was getting along with my stepdad less and less, so to rid myself of the emotional and physical clutter, I needed to break out. But trying to move out and fund a rap career meant that I needed fast money—apparently half naked in stilettos. Still, it wasn't like they were kicking me out of the house and dancing was my only choice. No, I chose to be there, though I quickly regretted it. The irony of it all was that I hated moving my body so much that I actually failed gym class in high school. I had to go to summer school for it in order to get my high school diploma. Now I was being paid to move my body with no clothes on. I still can't even really comprehend how I found myself dancing in the Bronx. I'd met this one girl out in Philly who brought the idea to my attention. She asked me, "Have you ever danced before?" I was like, "No, but what's that like?" I didn't even need to wait for her response because all I saw were dollar signs in my head. It just sounded like easy money, so I started dancing in Philly. Well, for one night, until one of my homies found out. He was like, "Yo, I heard you're dancing now?" I'd already been spotted by *somebody*, so after that I was like, "Welp, I guess I won't be dancing anymore in Philly. *That's* crazy." I knew I had to leave and go dance somewhere else if that was going to keep happening (which it totally would have). My mother didn't know this was going down *at all*. I somehow managed to keep this new double life of partial nudity tightly buttoned up. So that girl I met—my Strip Club Svengali—told me she was driving to the Golden Lady in the Bronx like once or twice a week with some other girls in a van. That sounds much shadier than it was. I still didn't really wanna do it, though. I knew that I needed some quick money, so that was the most alluring part about it. And I honestly didn't mind walking around naked and dancing by myself, but everything else just felt so annoying. I was the laziest stripper. I just didn't wanna do stuff. I didn't want to touch anybody, and I damn sure didn't want them to touch me. After I started getting positive feedback from my failed lap dances-turned-topless cyphers, I started hiding from the club owner. I didn't want to get on the pole. It was required to dance at the Golden Lady. Every dancer had a certain set time when they were supposed to get on the pole and dance. I didn't want to do that, so I would trade off my times with the other dancers. I needed as much individual time with the customers as possible to rap for them. My manager hated me. I hated him too, but I didn't hate the money.

I don't know how much money I really made while dancing, but judging by the thickness of the stack of bills every night, it was a lot to me. I really liked having money to buy myself things—just trivial shit that to a teenager felt like essentials. I felt like I was too damn old to be broke. I grew up in an environment where money was an issue. Where tokens for the bus had to be saved up for, and jackets and shoes required a whole conversation before I could purchase either (and rarely both at once). I didn't want to live like that as I approached adulthood. I wanted more, at warp speed. And when the money arrived, I've gotta admit it was pretty exciting. My favorite thing to do with my dancing money was head to this one jazz spot in Philly with my friend, where they played live music and had the best food! I felt like such a grown-up, ballin' with my earnings, when I knew I should be saving them like I had planned to do in the first place. But it's hard when you're a teenager who had to struggle with money as a child and now it's right there in your face. That urgency to leave my home wasn't as overpowering as it could've been, mainly because I didn't actually have to leave. The fun lasted for about a month and a half, until depression set in. I started to feel stuck, like I was heading down a road to fucking up my life. I knew I didn't fit in from the first day I put them heels on, and eventually the "joke" of it wore off. My conscience seeing other women struggling to make ends meet was one thing, and being separated from my purpose was another. Even the customers knew I didn't belong there. Nobody wants to watch the sad stripper dance.

A few regulars told me I should leave once they heard me rap. They were in a local crew in New York City called the Ruff Ryders, and a bunch of them rode around the city on motorcycles. Some of them even made music. "You really need to get the fuck up out of here," they'd tell me. I didn't know how. I also didn't know that a few years later they'd be the same guys who'd have my back while I was on the road touring. In that moment, they were just the precious few who kept reminding me of the bigger picture. Then one night, it all came together.

Musically, I was so focused on my own shit, but when it came to who was taking over the rap game, I lived under a rock. So when Ma$e came into the club, that meant nothing to me, even though everyone else was so excited. He was the new Bad Boy, after all. I still didn't know what that meant. I mean, I knew who Puff Daddy was, but his new artist he'd just signed? Nope. One of the older girls came up to me and said, "You need to go dance for Ma$e. You're around his age." Ugh, fine.

I walked up to him and said, "Hey, do you want a dance?" He probably saw the enthusiasm on my face. "What's your name?" he asked. I might've been Mystique or Mystery that week. Some shit. He was like, "No, what's your *real* name?" My defense mode kicked in. "Why are you asking? I don't know you!" I snapped. He was calm and he was polite. "Yo, man, chill out," he said in his very distinctive Ma$e voice. "Go get a chair and come sit down." I was puzzled. "What? Why?" He kept cutting through my extra-ness with calmness. "Tell me about yourself. What do you want to do with your life?" he continued. "Why do *you* care?" was my answer. I couldn't stop being extra, because even though it was one of the quietest nights at the Golden Lady, I didn't need a therapy session with my shirt off and a thong on.

I started to see on his face that there was a sincerity to him. "I'm serious," he said. "What do you *really* want to do with your life?" Somehow, he got through to me. "I want to rap," I said. "That's what I really wanna do." He asked to hear me rap, and so I did. He smiled at me. "Let me hear something else," he added. And I gave him some more. He responded, "Okay, why don't you get dressed?" My extraness started brewing again as I asked him why. "Why don't you just come with me? We can ride around and even go to the studio." I knew he was famous, but I most definitely wasn't going to be some murder headline on the news, so I said to him, "Nah, you ain't takin' me by myself! I have to take my friends with me." It wasn't like one or two girls, either. It was like four chicks—we all danced together at the club. Since the night was slow, they all left too to come with me. Ma$e didn't care. He said, "Aight, cool. My peoples is with me. You ride in the car with me, and your girls can ride in the car with him." That was good enough for me, so I got dressed and got in the car with Ma$e.

We spent the night playing beats and driving through the city, rapping in his car. It was the lyrical exercise that I needed in my life, and it was the most fun I'd had in New York City since I started dancing there. At one point, he even stopped at Puffy's house to pick up some money, and I just knew that I couldn't go back to my old life. "If you really want this, I mean *really* want it, then you need to stop dancing," he said. "Now." I already knew, but I needed to hear it from someone else. We rapped until the sun came up, and Ma$e told my girls and I, "You might as well just spend the night." He brought us to his sister Stason's house to sleep, and by the time we woke up, he was gone. I never returned to the Golden Lady after that car ride with Ma$e. We didn't even exchange numbers, but something told me I would see him again. And I did, a few years later.

I was at Puffy's restaurant Justin's in New York one night when Ma$e showed up. He saw me and ran up to me, grabbed me by the arm and pulled me to the side. "What are you doing in New York! What's up with you?" He sounded more concerned than curious. I was proud to answer those questions—no extra-ness needed. "I'm signed to the Ruff Ryders!" I told him. He was so happy. Once I started recording my debut album, he came to so many of the sessions just to support me and watch it all go down. When I later found out Ma$e became a pastor, I was not the least bit shocked. I knew he could change people's lives with his words and messaging, because he one hundred percent changed mine. There's this thing about receiving messages from a higher power, where anyone can be tapped in to send the message, but you have to be open to receiving it. I'm just glad I was ready to hear it that night, and Ma$e was the right person to deliver it.

Out of everything I learned in those two months of dancing, the thing that sticks out most is the repercussions that dancing can have on a woman's life and career. It follows you for a long time. Sometimes forever. To this day, I'm still asked about it, and I'm like, "Are you serious? After a whole career, this is still what you're asking about?" It's not like I'm ashamed of it; it just wasn't my path and it wasn't for me. Once I was signed though, I knew that I had to be the one to address it head-on. It wasn't going to be that secret that someone would hold over me and then reveal to the world without my consent. So for my very first cover story with *XXL Magazine,* I had to be the one to bring it up to the interviewer to take the power out of it. I really didn't want it to come bite me in my ass down the road, and I definitely didn't want anyone else to bring it up for me. I also had to prepare my mother for the big reveal when it went to print, because she still didn't even know I'd danced. She found out the day the magazine hit the stands. I called her up and said, "Mom, I need you to read this article and then call me so we can talk about it." After she read it, she called me back. I was surprised she wasn't mad at me; she understood why I'd done it. She knew I'd wanted to make money and was already suspicious when I was just randomly going back and forth from Philly to New York City.

"I knew something was going on at that time," she told me, "because you were just different. You just didn't seem happy." She was right. These days when I hit the strip club, I'm much happier as a proud customer.

4

ON THE EVE OF DESTRUCTION

I held a gun for the first time when I was eight years old. It was a pearl-handled .25 and it belonged to my aunt Karen. Sometimes I'd carefully hold the gun and just look at it when we were together. My aunt Karen was just a teenager when she started selling drugs, and I became her little helper. I wasn't on the block dealing at eight or something, but I would count the caps on the crack vials for her by color: red, blue and so on. I also knew the price tag attached to each cap color. Some kids used flash cards, but I had these. Even as a teen, my aunt Karen had a swag about her, one that I would eventually emulate and evolve into my rap persona. She was definitely a hustler, but not some high-level criminal; she wanted to make money just like I did when I eventually got to the age she was then. We didn't have a lot of money growing up, and opportunities to make it weren't within reach as a teen. She did what she had to do. And Aunt Karen could *dress*; I'm talking about all the designers that anyone cared about in the '80s. She even had me dipped in Adidas Ti sweat suits and Gucci link earrings too. Since we were close enough in age that she was like my big sister, I got to hang around her and all of her friends. I felt so cool.

Aunt Karen never left me behind, though years later when she passed away, I felt guilty that I'd maybe left her. I was thirty-two and in LA when I got the call. Aunt Karen had some health issues, yet she continued to do her thing with drinking and smoking. Her body gave in with a seizure, and I felt so far away from Philly in that moment. I wished I had paid more attention to her health scares, or urged her to go see some specialists, anything I could think of. Maybe she wouldn't have listened, but at least I could have tried harder. This was the woman who gave me holidays when I didn't have them, and brought our family together with gatherings and barbecues. She was the glue, and while she gave me my edge, she also helped give me my heart. To this day when I hit the stage, I turn on my inner Aunt Karen, though now, channeling her spirit has a whole different meaning with her not being here. I still talk to her though, and she talks back in her own subtle ways. That knack for subtlety is also something that I have infused into my rap persona.

Every rapper has one, and if they say, "Nah, this is just how I am," then they're probably lying. There's a switch we flip when the cameras turn on, and it doesn't matter if you're a rapper, an actor, an athlete or a pop star—we all have one. In becoming and staying "Eve," I had to learn when and where to put my superhero cape on and transform, for my own survival. It's still a work in progress. Coming from battle rap, I didn't know how to properly hold a microphone when I first started performing actual full songs. As a battle rapper, you instinctively hold your mic higher to your mouth, which may help you get your insults out harder, but won't help when you're in a stadium with an audience who just wants to hear your song exactly how it sounds on the radio. I grew into my artistry by understanding that you're *supposed* to grow with it. I knew how to write bars but had to learn how to write songs. I also had to stop looking at just rappers onstage and start observing pop stars and rock musicians, even jazz players, to study the art of not only hitting a stage but *owning* it. I've performed through panic attacks, the flu, food poisoning—where I'd get off the stage and puke right after. I've lost my voice completely, and had to get cortisone shots in my butt to open up my vocals for one hour to perform before they'd close back up again. In my eyes, sometimes you've gotta do what you've gotta do. So yeah, people can leave you alone with some tea and some soup and a nap, but after that you have to kind of get to it. For me, it's no different from being an athlete with a ripped Achilles' heel still finishing a game. Maybe that's why I feel so at home on the stage—because I've put so much of myself on it. It's still one of my favorite places in the world, next to being with my son. But that all took time. That E-V-E though? The pit bull in a skirt? She's my superhero. The one part of it all that has stayed the same, though, is me: Eve Jihan, the woman behind that superhero cape just checking for the next phone booth to enter into to transform. Funnily enough, though, most of the me that the world ended up seeing developed before I even signed a record deal.

I called myself "Eve of Destruction" because my name was Eve and I thought the movie title sounded cool. It's as simple as that. It was probably the flyest battle rap name, especially for a girl. In the tenth grade, I chopped off all of my hair and bleached what was left blonde. It took a minute to perfect the color for me. The first time was so terrible. It came out looking like cinnamon toast, and I was so mad. So I kept bleaching it and bleaching it and bleaching it until it got to the color that I wanted. I entered into the music industry with that hairdo, but over time I tried to change up the color, especially as I moved on to each new project. "Red from blonde, yeah bitch, I'm drastic." So drastic that the first time I dyed my hair red, I tried to perm it on the same day, and it all broke off. This was entering into my *Scorpion* album, and I had grown out my hair, so I had to cut it short again. I guess that was symbolic. Like I said, a work in progress.

As for the paw print tattoos? I got those before I signed to Ruff Ryders. I was in the Bronx with my friend one night, drinking a mai tai, and I don't even know how I wound up getting those paw prints. I think it was a dare. One of the girls in Total had paw prints tattooed on her thigh, and I loved those, so I wanted them too. My friend said, "Oh, you should get them on your chest. That would be so dope." Then I took it and ran with it, apparently. It worked out once I joined the Ruff Ryders because DMX was obsessed with dogs and all of the young writers and rappers in Ruff Ryders were called "pups," so it all made sense on a brand level. A lot of people thought I got those tattoos when I signed, but nope, those came with me when I got my record deal. I remember when my mother first saw them, she was so annoyed. I'm sure she thought, "What the hell are you doing with your life?" I mean, it was a fair question. At one point later on in my career, I entertained

the idea of getting them removed, and then my mom told
me I couldn't because they were how people know me now.
She finally came around to my paw prints, just as I thought
I was done with them. Some actually think I paint them
on too. One time, an elderly woman asked to touch them.
Aren't people so interesting?

It does make me smile though when I see girls with paw
print tattoos, or who bleach their hair blonde and cut it
short. My only advice to you all is don't dye your hair and
perm it on the same day. Really, though, none of this was
planned except for my ambition. I was just a girl trying to
find her place in the world, one rhyme at a time, though I
hit some false starts along the way.

Once I stopped dancing, I was on track to figure out
my career in a different way, and NYU was back on the
table. I was ready to pursue that degree in Special Effects
Makeup, so I found myself back in New York City and
ready to start my application for school (which ironically
never happened). But after Ma$e basically changed my life
in one night, I knew I had to keep music somewhere at the
forefront, even if I was going to school too. I wasn't going
to let all of that valuable time in New York go to waste,
especially when it was the mecca for hip-hop at the time.
So I did what any completely sane individual would do: I
stalked music industry executives. My favorite person to
harass was Mark Pitts. Back then he had just left Bad Boy
and started Mark Pitts Management (it's called ByStorm
Entertainment now), and I would literally pull up to his
office with my demo and just sit there, waiting for him to
listen to my tape. I did this almost every single day. Eventually, I became an office fixture. I don't even know what
I had hoped would happen if I did that—maybe that I'd

get signed or get a super high-level manager. I was just so determined to make *something* work and really didn't want to move backwards.

Mark liked my music, but nothing materialized beyond the intensity of my own ambitions. I needed something to happen somewhere, and just when I was about to lose hope again, it did. After two months of dancing and two months of plotting my next moves, I received a phone call that changed my life. Up until that point, I didn't *really* have a manager, even though I wanted one (hence my Mark Pitts stalking sessions). There would always be some random drug dealer or street dude ready to help me out with *something*, but never a legitimate person whose purpose was to represent and advocate for me. So one day my homegirl called me and said, "These two dudes wanna know if you still rap." I mean, I *did*, but I had sort of resolved that maybe it wasn't going to happen on the timeline I'd had in mind since I was fourteen. "Yeah, I do. Why, wassup?" was my reply. She told me these dudes wanted to get in touch with me because Dr. Dre's right-hand man was coming through town. "Can I give them your number?" she asked me. "Yeah," I said. I mean, what could it hurt? I was a massive fan of Dr. Dre's. I'd smoke weed and listen to N.W.A. and *The Chronic* all throughout high school, so I was masking more enthusiasm than I cared to admit, but I had to protect myself from disappointment. These dudes may never call me, and I had to brace myself for that. They did, though, and immediately laid down this elaborate plan. They were coming to pick me up and bring me to where this man was staying. It was Mike Lynn, Dre's right-hand man, just like my homegirl had said. "He don't know you're coming there to audition," they told me. Great. "So just go with it." We showed up to this house, and Mike thinks I'm the weed girl here to sell him something. I was selling him *something*, but it wasn't a dime bag. Once we walked in, the dudes started playing a beat and I just start rapping my ass off. Mike is standing there like *What the fuck?* Once I stopped rapping, one of the dudes, named Marc Byers, tells Mike, "Look, I know you didn't wanna hear anyone else, but she's *really* good." Mike agreed with Marc. He said to me, "Nah, you're like really dope." So dope that he called Dr. Dre right on the spot and said, "I think we've found our girl." By the end of that week, I was on a flight to Los Angeles.

As soon as the plane landed on a Friday, I was studio-bound with the producer Mel-Man to cut my demo. It was a self-titled song called "Eve of Destruction." We recorded, mixed and mastered it within the span of like three days, and it was later put on the soundtrack to the film *Bulworth*. I thought that I'd *made it*. Like, *See? I told you all I needed was the right opportunity and I'd be blowin' up.* There I was, with the first demo that I actually cut and it gets put right on a soundtrack. When I said on the song, "I'm in LA now with Dre now, ain't comin' back 'cause I'm stuck," I really believed that. I thought I was perfectly fine, and in one whirlwind weekend in LA, I was where I had hoped to be all along.

A lot happened in a short amount of time. We cut the demo, I got signed, I flew back home and had a going-away party, and then I was right back in LA, ready to be the First Lady of Dre's Aftermath Entertainment. It all felt so surreal. When I first pulled up to Dr. Dre's home, it looked like a fuckin' castle. I thought I had arrived and was living the dream. Aftermath set me up with my own bank account (At Wells Fargo! A real, legit bank!), which I never had before, and I had a two-bedroom condo in the Valley that was amazing. I had my own place, after feeling *so* crowded at home for *so* long. I had money at my disposal from my advance, and I was ready to pursue my path to stardom, LA-style.

I'll tell you this: once I hit the West Coast, it was a total culture shock. That East Coast/West Coast difference is *real*. I came with my own built-in set of expectations, though, for myself, the LA experience and my life as a signed rapper. I really thought I was going to land directly onto the set of a John Singleton film or West Coast rap video. And you know what? Most of what I'd imagined was true. We had some gang shit on the East Coast, but it's nothing like how the West Coast moves. The Bloods, the Crips…it was so far removed from places like New York City, but even more removed from Philly. I remember watching movies like *Boyz n the Hood* and thinking, "Why do they have on shorts, a hoodie and flip-flops? Why do they even dress like that?" I then wondered what the actual temperature in Los Angeles even was. The things that kept me up at night… After getting there and living there awhile, I completely got it. The climate is perfectly conducive to some shorts and a hoodie…and also some flip-flops.

I definitely turned my condo into a real-life music video set, throwing these wild-ass parties. We were living the "Nuthin' but a 'G' Thang" music video up in there. When I would pop into other artists' studio sessions, it was a hurricane of weed, fried chicken and dominos. I loved that about being in LA. Even when I was fortunate enough to get into the studio to record, it was with these well-known West Coast producers (like Mel-Man, who went on to help produce songs for Dre like "Still D.R.E.," "Forgot About Dre,"

"Role Model" and "The Next Episode" among so many others) and I got to see artists and groups like Tha Dogg Pound all the time because of their affiliation with Dre. The vibe they all created gave me something I never had before. I was moving in circles with people I would see on award shows or hear on the radio, and the experience felt so different. My main feeling, though, was: "How come this isn't moving fast enough?" I didn't want to just *meet* these kinds of people; I wanted to *be* them. I wanted to be their peer.

I spent around eight months in LA, and in my mind, I didn't accomplish what I wanted to at all. I felt myself just hanging around and waiting. I watched Dre prioritize other artists like Eminem, who was also newly signed and working on his Aftermath debut, *The Slim Shady LP*. "Where was my album?" I thought, constantly. Then the Philly jumped right out of me, and I started pulling up to other artists' studio sessions trying to get my moment. They knew I was good—great, in fact—so what was the problem? I'd literally just show up to a random session like, "Okay, so when do I record? Am I gonna get to record too? Where's my studio time?" I guess you could say that my timeline and Dre's timeline were not in sync at all (to say the least), and it wasn't long before he was completely annoyed by me. He didn't see the investment potential because he was too invested in other artists. He left me high and dry.

And then it happened: I received a phone call from someone in Dre's camp, breaking the news to me that I had been dropped from Aftermath. He didn't even call me himself. I just felt so deflated and dismissed, by Dr. Dre of all people. That flight home was horrible. I didn't know what to do or what to say to anyone back home. Even though it was just for a short time, I had been in LA, in my own place, living my own life as a recording artist with a song on a soundtrack. Now I was flying right back home to move back in with my mom. Depression set in quickly, and I wouldn't leave the house. I couldn't find the words to tell anyone what had really happened and how fast it had been taken away from me. It was the kind of failure that I never thought I'd experience, but I did. The highs and lows were frequent during that period.

Before I even got my Aftermath deal, though, Scott Storch had called me with an opportunity to record a verse for the Roots on their upcoming single "You Got Me." After loving the Roots for so long, this was such a big deal to me. Getting on a song with Black Thought, my rap crush? It was crazy. So I went to the studio and laid down my verse. I was also invited to come shoot the music video with them too, but when I got to the location there was no music video set. Somebody messed up (or somebody didn't want me there) and I was given the wrong address, and the shoot went on without me.

Months later, when the track released, my name wasn't even in the credits. Everyone thought it was Erykah Badu rapping. It was as if they figured "Who cares? She's un-signed," though in the span of recording that song and it releasing, I actually was unsigned, signed and then signed again. My absence from the video didn't help, either. My total disappointment from that whole experience later peaked in 2000, when the Roots won a Grammy Award for Best Rap Performance by a Duo or Group for that very song and I didn't, because my name wasn't credited on it. Years later, Questlove tried to give me his Grammy for the song when I appeared on *Late Night with Jimmy Fallon*, but his was broken in half and by then I had my own Grammy.

I definitely didn't need (or want) his broken one. Talk about an awkward moment, but I think the whole Roots crew knew they had collectively messed up.

That feeling of being anonymous was hard for me to shake when that situation first happened, especially when it was timed nearly perfectly with being dropped by my record label. Disappointments shouldn't happen that close together, if you ask me. But they had. I was fortunate, though, because Marc Byers was still riding with me, and he became my manager. At that point I didn't really know what he was managing. That feeling of being at a standstill was about to settle in yet again, when I got a call from Marc: "We're heading to Yonkers."

5

THE PIT BULL IN A SKIRT

DMX never called me Eve. He called me *Evenin'*, which actually made sense since the way he acted with me versus the fellas was like night and day.

He would greet me in that DMX growl, like he was barking military orders at me, yet somehow at the same time saluting me. "EVENIN'!" he'd shout in his lovingly aggressive tone. I can still hear him saying it now.

There were multiple sides to X, but mainly he had two modes. There was Earl (the name he was born with) and then there was DMX. There was an innocence to Earl, which might sound crazy, but it's true, and at times even when he was drunk he would have these moments of clarity, where you'd just think, "Where the hell did *that* come from?" Probably the same place his lyrical genius and the purity of the art that he created did. X's personality filled a room and (on the right day) made everyone so happy, as he'd pace around with his cup of "blood," which was basically a concoction made up of Hennessy, Red Passion Alizé, and some other stuff to give it that deep bloodred color. X was unique to say the least. He was always so full of energy, but he also *loved* to sleep—so much so that he would get unreasonably angry whenever anyone woke him up.

Except for me.

I never felt the wrath of X like everyone else did. I definitely witnessed the best and worst sides of him, but the latter was never pointed at me. He was always so sweet to me and gave the best hugs. The guys would always have me be the one to wake him up from a nap or break any bad or disappointing news to him. I think it was because they knew X would be a little gentler with me. If he would ever try to scream at me or throw shit like he did with the guys, they also knew that I could handle him and anyone else.

I think I proved that from Day One.

After a few months of mourning my Aftermath situation (and considering that NYU route one more time), I got the call from Marc that Jimmy Iovine had reached out to him. The Yonkers crew that he was working with, the Ruff Ryders (ironically signed to the same parent company, Interscope, that I'd just been dropped from), were looking for a female emcee to join their crew. They wanted me to audition for them. It was go time...yet again. I knew I had a mission at hand, and in many ways, it felt like this could be my last chance. The stakes are different for women in this game. When it comes to being given pep talks, you're told "you got this" instead of "there will be more opportunities"—in essence, your pep talk is about resilience rather than having confidence in the abundance of options waiting for you on the other side if something doesn't pan out. With very few exceptions, I had to give *myself* a lot of my pep talks before I joined the Ruff Ryders. I was my own voice of reason, telling myself to keep going, even when I was clouded with doubts about the outcome. That's not always easy to do, even if you know you're destined for what you're chasing.

Either way, this was the new opportunity that I had, and I was gonna take it head-on. I was ready to leave Yonkers as a Ruff Ryder whether these dudes recognized it or not. I knew some of them individually a little bit from the Golden Lady, but not as a whole organized unit. And when I lived in LA, I would hang around some of the guys whenever they were out West, since I craved that Northeast sense of community. Mel-Man first introduced me to DMX. He said to me, "Yo, they got this kid from New York who's blowin' up." Then I met him a few times and he seemed absolutely insane, but really cool. I didn't really know too much about the rest of the crew collectively. All I knew was that they were pretty big in Yonkers and Harlem. And they were fun: a bunch of guys who loved rapping and motorcycles and dogs. But what they lacked was some divine feminine energy to balance out all the barking. I knew I could provide that while still keeping it gangster.

The ride from Philly to Yonkers was stressful. I wouldn't exactly say I was *nervous*; *determined* is more like it. My manager and I really laid down what needed to be done when I got there, so having a game plan helped keep my anxiety from taking over. But again, I couldn't help but feel like this was a "do or die" situation.

We were told to come to the official Ruff Ryders studio, called Power House. DMX used to say it was where "the dogs get trained." They built that Yonkers studio from the ground up, and there was a lot of heart in there. See, the story of the Ruff Ryders dates back to the late '80s, when Darrin Dean (we called him Dee) and his brother Joaquin Dean (we called him Waah) started their own company. They were in the streets pretty heavy and funneled that work into a record label to stay out of trouble. Their goal was always to help artists, but also to keep them off the streets—they knew better than most people that they weren't the best place to be. So they'd see guys like the Lox around the way when they were younger and pass them money and sneakers so they wouldn't hustle to get them, all while they kept building and building their empire. X was their first artist, but they had major plans in place.

It took almost ten years for everything to actually take off for them, but when it did, it *really did*. And on top of the music, there was a whole crew of Ruff Ryders who rode motorcycles together in packs. I'm talking about dudes from all corners of the world, claiming the name and riding their bikes, reppin' the Double R. Even years later, when I was on tour, I'd get approached by random dudes who would say to me, "We're Ruff Ryders, so anything you need, we got you." No matter where I was, if a Ruff Ryder was in the building, then I was taken care of. In that sense, it was like a real kinship, and the deeper you were a part of it all, the more they became like your family. I always loved that about them, and for a girl like me who was still figuring out my own sense of community in hip-hop, they were the home I didn't know I needed.

I remember first pulling up to the studio. It was in this redbrick building, and when you stepped inside there were multiple rooms. Some rooms looked really dark, but then others were contrasted with this really bright "ghetto fancy" shade of teal. Every room with those bright walls looked like some Midwestern kitchen in an '80s sitcom. The one constant, though, was that there were dudes *everywhere*. I knew so many of them, too, so I wasn't walking in like some new girl. There were a lot of "wassups" being exchanged, and a lot of familiar faces, which helped. I don't really know if they all knew what I was there for, but maybe they did. Maybe they knew that I was going to be the girl who made the cypher complete. I walked into this one big room, the arena basically, and it was full of more guys and a bunch of pit bulls. I couldn't really tell who I was auditioning for more: the men or the dogs. But my assignment was to battle every man who rapped in that room. I was ready.

I knew one thing was clear going in: I couldn't take my usual battle rap approach that I used with the guys back in West Philly. Little-dick jokes weren't gonna land with these dudes. Since I knew my strengths (and freestyling definitely ain't one of them), I had already spent some time perfecting my rhymes for them without even knowing what I'd be using them for. It didn't matter; it felt like I was rapping for my life regardless. I walked to the center and my first opponents came forward.

I think it was Drag-On and Infa Red who stepped to me first. Other guys like Cross were waiting to go next. And what happened after that? Well, I don't really know, because I kind of blacked out. Words came out of me, but I was consumed by the moment. I don't remember what I said or who it was even aimed at—all I know is that when I came to, everyone was cheering like *OH SHIT!!!* Waah and Dee had their nephew Swizz Beatz apprenticing as a producer, and he ran into that room, bouncing up and down. I just kind of stood there and surveyed the room and everyone cheering, like I was some self-possessed Shaolin master who'd just annihilated a temple full of opponents and was assessing the damage. Their mouths were open, but my mind processed nothing. Maybe it was shock? I knew I'd just done something, though, and I guess it was good.

Waah looked at me and said, "Welcome to Ruff Ryders."

You would think that in that moment, my confidence would've hopped in the driver's seat like, "I told you!"

It didn't.

Insecurity stepped in instead. You could call it impostor syndrome, or maybe it was the fact that I was *so* immune to good news at that point, but I wasn't sure I had it in me. That's when Waah and Dee sat me down and said, "Yes, you do." Waah was the first to really see my potential and knew that I could grow into the artist I wanted to be. Dee was the motivator, my coach. Their positions were fixed in those first days of me signing to Ruff Ryders: they stayed that way throughout my journey with them. They helped me stay the course, even when I was trailing off.

There was a lot that drew me to the Ruff Ryders that, in spite of my own insecurities, made me feel like it was meant to be. For one, I knew so many of them—and even when I danced, the Ruff Ryder guys that showed up to the club were also the same guys telling me I shouldn't be at the club at all. Another reason was that the Deans were Muslim. I was always drawn to Islam, so that part just made sense. Waah and Dee's sister Chivon Dean was also a part of the label, and having a woman there gave me this added layer of protection—where I knew everything was cool because a woman (in power) was present. But at the heart of it was the fact that they all *really* believed in me. They knew my worth on the mic and as a woman, and they respected me for it. I wouldn't realize just how important that was until later on.

Within a week of getting signed to Ruff Ryders, I left Philly for Yonkers for a little bit, then eventually moved deeper into New York City. By my first studio session, Waah had dubbed me "the pit bull in a skirt." Within like a month of me signing that deal, they already had me in X's "How's It Goin' Down" video, running through the spray of a fire hydrant, and then again in the video for "Ruff Ryder's Anthem." I was a part of the family, and I was more than ready to finally start my career. My first introduction as a Ruff Ryder was going to be on the remix of "Ruff Ryder's Anthem," but before that? Boot camp.

X wasn't lying when he said the dogs had to be trained. They called all of us young rappers "the pups," and they weren't going to let us just hop on a song and act like we all knew what the fuck we were doing when we didn't. There was a real purpose to that remix. First of all, it was on DJ Clue?'s *The Professional*, one of the first *major* releases from a world-renowned DJ, a mixtape released by a legit major label and not sold out of the trunk of a car with a photo-copied cover. That alone raised the bar, but then it was also our big introduction. The Lox were with us now, I was there, Swizz was producing, Drag was there and of course X was there… I mean, it was a big deal. This was their Ruff Ryders moment—it was no longer just DMX and a bunch of promises. We were a unit, and we were announcing our arrival. From an internal business standpoint, though, it was the litmus test to see who the public gravitated toward.

The irony is that all of those sessions in the studio didn't even lead to my verse on the remix. The real genesis of that verse happened right outside of the Apollo, in Dee's SUV.

I wrote a lot in the car, just because we were always on the move, and that verse in particular will forever stay in my memory—especially since it was my big introduction. It was like, how do you combine the spirit of a battle rapper with the charisma of a pop star? That was what I was after, so I polished up my verse and let it fly.

When the song finally arrived, it spread like wildfire. The streets were feeling that anthem, and even more, they were feeling *me*! I was brand-new to the rap world, even though for me it'd felt like forever in the making. I remember I was in Harlem when I first heard the song blasting through the speakers of a car. I couldn't believe it. I was on the radio. There was no turning back now. I was officially the First Lady of the Ruff Ryders.

That little test of who the public would love basically revealed that it was all of us, but for different reasons. We were putting together our first compilation album, *Ryde or Die Vol. 1*, and by that point, everyone wanted to hear what we had to say. When the album dropped, it went right to number one, and like two months later, it went platinum. Mission accomplished. We were here.

I had a lot of shine on that first project, showing up on some of the posse cuts like "Ryde or Die," but then getting to sing the hook for Jay-Z's "Jigga My Nigga" and then getting my own solo songs, like "Do That Shit" and "What Y'all Want." I think everyone knew that "What Y'all Want" was the one.

That song was like my little love letter to New York City, a shout-out to my new home. I used to go to this club Jimmy's in the Bronx and get tipsy and try to dance merengue (you definitely couldn't get me to do that sober) while all the Dominican guys yelled "Rubia! Rubia!" which means "blonde-haired girl" in Spanish. I'd be like, "Yeah, I don't speak Spanish. Sorry." That's why I open the song with, "Rubia, huh! Papi screamin' outta they mouth." It was also a perfect entry point for that beat being what it was, having such a strong Latin influence. That track, though, was my first real lesson in song structure. These bars weren't gonna be in the cypher or wedged between everyone else's bars. This was gonna be just me on the radio. The stakes were even higher than my very first song I released with Dre, because now I was representing a whole army. Like Waah had said and I declared in the song, I was the pit bull in a skirt.

I kept my lyrics strong, but made sure it sounded like a complete song, even singing the hook with Nokio from Dru Hill. The funniest part about that whole song process was the music video. The guys got me a dance teacher, and he *hated* me. He's the one I'm dancing with in the video. It was all Dee's fault. He was like, "You need to get salsa classes." I was like, "WHY?! It's a *video!*" Dee said, "Nah. I got this idea. I'm telling you, it's gonna be cool because no one else is doing it." So he picked the meanest dance instructor to ever cha-cha. He barely spoke English, but he knew enough words to yell at me. I naturally wanted to lead in the dancing, and he would shout, "I lead!" Then he'd try to show me my feet were refusing to move backwards and go, "Look! Feet!" only with his heavy-ass Spanish accent, it sounded like he was saying *Luke feet*. I didn't know Spanish, but I knew how to say, "Bro, what the fuck? I've never done this before!"

It was such a big production, and I was so new to it all. We rented out a night club in the Bronx for most of it, and had like an eight-piece band with hired dancers. When they told me Fat Joe was going to make a cameo in my video, I was so excited. I was like, "What? Fat Joe is gonna be in *my* video?!" It was all such a big deal to me, and the first time I felt like people were investing in me and my career. I really felt like a star, even with all of the rough parts of putting that video together. That shoot day is vividly burned into my memory. I remember getting my hair braided, and then getting dressed in the back of a car. One of the guys' girlfriends helped style and dress me for it. We also shot parts of that video in the middle of the night, on the steps of the Met with water shooting at me. *That* was a challenge, mainly because we didn't have permission to use the museum's steps—it was like a big rush so that we didn't all get arrested. I also got to show off my motorbike riding skills (on the quad) in those street shots. I *was* a Ruff Ryder, after all. The whole thing was so gangster, but it was also glam. Just like me.

The guys knew that song had to be a single. It sounded different, and I looked different from any of the girls that were doing their thing. I don't really know if there was a full-blown strategy behind the production aspect, but for me as an artist? I was standing out. I was forging my own path in the game, and the guys helped me with that vision. I hadn't spent all of that time just to be another pretty face out there. I had to be unique. Once that happened, and the world was receptive to it, there was only one thing left to do.

It was time to drop my debut album.

6

GIRL FIGHT

I used to lie and tell people that Will Smith was my cousin. I don't really know what I was hoping to gain from that. Maybe a head start in the game? A connection to greatness through familial ties? I don't even know. I later heard a rumor that Will Smith had a sister who also rapped and nobody ever got to hear about her. So if his own sister couldn't blow up with her brother's name behind her, then what the hell was his so-called cousin gonna get?

Being the only girl in a sea of dudes is lonely. That whole First Lady title is cool and all, but once I entered into the music industry as the First Lady of the Ruff Ryders, I thought all of the first ladies hung out. I pictured this big sisterhood, full of us girls just sharing war stories and tips and being a support system and cheering section for each other. I didn't expect us all to climb trees into a clubhouse, but maybe brunch? Something?

Yeah, not exactly. Actually, not even a little bit. I got knocked into reality really quickly, but I needed that check early. I was so young and so naive. And I was also such a nerd about it all. I was like twenty years old and couldn't contain my excitement. I was really just happy to be there, finally making music and releasing it. In LA with Aftermath, I felt like a spectator, watching it all go down and sometimes being invited into the circle. I had everything that teenage me needed right in front of me—money, weed, a home, fun—but no album to show for it. Even worse, I found myself popping into rooms and asking when it was going to be my turn, but that turn never came. It humbled me in a way that changed my whole perspective the second time around. I started to see it as the universe giving me a trial run on the road to greatness. I received the message and saw my new opportunity as my do-over, and in the place where I was supposed to be from the beginning.

Once I became a Ruff Ryder, I was signed, but at that point with the crew it wasn't like an Aftermath-style signing with all of the bells and whistles. I had no bank account, and I didn't really have any money. I was bouncing around, living in different places. At one point, I was staying in an extended-stay hotel in New Jersey, so I was basically homeless, living out of a bag and eating chips from the hotel vending machine. I relied on Dee a lot for money. The money wasn't flowing, but my faith was, and the big difference from my Aftermath days was that I was able to record in the studio. They'd pick me up from the hotel or wherever else I was staying, drive me right to the studio—where I'd spend the day and night writing—and then drop me right back off. Every single day. For the first time, I felt *in* it and a part of it. I was now *in the circle*, but that came with me learning how to act.

Now I was in rooms with my absolute heroes, my favorite artists. It was an adjustment. This one time I was heading into the studio with N.O.R.E., and when I got into the elevator, Busta Rhymes walked in with me. I couldn't speak. I'd been a fan since his days in Leaders of the New School, and instead of letting him know that (or even just introducing myself), I just stood there in silence in the elevator. He looked over at me and had no clue who I was. Then I realized we were both headed to the same place. Great. As we both walked into the studio, N.O.R.E. said to Busta, "This is that new girl!" and Busta was like, "Oh, *you're* the new girl!" I stood there shy like, "Yeaaaah that's meeee." See? Nerd.

The cool part about those early days was that so many people were just genuinely excited for me. I'd be up in Harlem with the guys a lot and you could feel the excitement there, or I'd go home to Philly and everyone there was like my aunt, uncle, or cousin. They really repped for me like I was the pride of the city. One thing about Philadelphians is that they always support their homegrown talent. I'd walk down the street and people would stop me to tell me how proud they were of me. They still do that when I'm in Philly. It's beautiful, and it's happened since the very beginning. So it was nothing to me, then, to assume all of the girls in rap were just sharing in the excitement of the moment. Like, can't we all just party like it's 1999—because it *actually is* 1999? Nope.

This wasn't a scarcity situation, either. I entered into an era of the music industry where so many women were out there thriving. We had the girls from the '80s still making music, the girls from the early to mid-'90s absolutely killing it, and here we were at the end of the '90s, getting to all be out there doing our thing at the same time. It wasn't like there was just one spot to be filled; there was room for all of us. At least that's how I felt. But that highly competitive mindset can be locked in sometimes, so when a new girl enters the scene, it's more like, "What's *she* doing here?" instead of "Come on over and join us!"

I tried. I really did. Maybe *too* hard. I'd run up to the girls and introduce myself like, "Hi! I'm Eve! I'm with the Ruff Ryders! Blah blah blah," and some of the girls would just look at me like, "Uh, are you okay?" It probably didn't help that I wasn't from around there. I mean, I was the girl from Philly. I might as well have been from a totally different planet, even though I was basically from next door. Style-wise, I looked nothing like the other girls. I had my short platinum blonde hair, and I'd wear my baggy jeans and Timbs but still be kind of girly. I entered into a world that was very split, where one side of the girls was dressing super sexy and the other wore strictly baggy clothes. I kind of kept it down the middle, I think, like only a few of the other girls. I'm sure some girls probably found that annoying too, how I wasn't purposely dressing one way or the other. How you saw me was exactly how I entered the scene—from my hair to my makeup to my clothes. I looked the same way as I had in high school. And it worked—for everyone but my peers.

After spending so much time battling men, it really just didn't click to me that women would be my competition in this. I know that might sound naive, but I didn't want to be competing with the girls. I was out for blood with the guys, though. I didn't want to be just a girl who could rap; I wanted to be seen as a great rapper. So why would the girls to my right and to my left be trying to fight me instead of the men trying to hold us back? It just felt so aggressive and unnecessary.

Don't get me wrong, I made some amazing friends who held me down and really rode for me, like Missy Elliott and later on Trina when she came out. They were my friends, and so were the few other rap girls that I would hang out with a lot. Lauryn Hill was wonderful; I got to meet her for the first time in Jamaica at a Bob Marley tribute show, and she was so nice to me when I went to visit her in her trailer during the concert. Queen Latifah was great, Salt-N-Pepa were too, as well as MC Lyte, and even girls like Amil and Solé. Lil' Kim and I got off to a rocky start, but now I can totally understand why. I was doing too much. I was such a fan of hers, and when I met her, I approached her like one. That wasn't the move. And even though there were so many of us, we were still really all fighting for that same little corner in the room. Kim had her guard up, so imagine how I looked being like, "Hi! I can't wait to get you on my record!" Years later, though, she and I finally connected, and we really got along. I loved her. I still do. We'd talk about having Yorkies; we even ended up on a Missy song together with Trina years later. But not all of the girls were great to me. Some said they were gonna have me blackballed (for what, I still don't know), while others thought they could use my two-month dancing stint as ammo (too late—I already talked about it). At one of my first big shows in Chicago, one of the girls pulled up and started yelling from the balcony, trying to mess up my show. She was carrying on from her seat like some heckler at the Apollo, yelling out her city (which, by the way, wasn't even Chicago) and trying to throw shit onto the stage. The battle rapper instantly came out of me. From the stage, I said to her (in the crowd), "Why don't you come onstage and let's battle?" I mean, clearly, if she had so much to say from her chair, she could say it standing up with a mic too, right? She left. Oh well. I think that was the turning point for me, when I realized that even if you aren't trying to compete, you're still in the race. All I wanted to do was stand out, really. I was disappointed by how some of the girls acted around me—even hurt by it.

It was sobering after coming in with this preconceived notion that the girls were gonna big-sis me. I remembered rolling blunts and smoking them in a hatchback back in Philly, quoting these girls' lines on their tracks word for word, and now I got to share space with them, only to have them give me the cold shoulder...or even worse. It's the reason why, even now, I will never turn down one of the new girls when they ask for advice. I'll jump on a track if I believe in the message. I've even come to meetings between women and their record labels when I sensed they were being bullied and didn't know what to ask for when it came to fighting back. I'll always be the big sis I didn't get to have in this, so they're not out there alone. This industry is not for the faint of heart, and I would rather help one of the new girls than pretend like I'm trying to compete with her.

My reputation following the "Ruff Ryder's Anthem" remix was growing. When the guys had the public decide who was going to be next based on their verses, it ended up being me, and once that decision was made, they were fast-tracking me to being a star. "What Y'all Want" only added to that excitement, especially once it hit number one on Billboard's Hot Rap Songs. Now I was in every conversation, people were asking me to collaborate, and I was doing fashion spreads and planning a whole album and music video rollout—all from one verse on a remix and one single off a compilation album. I can see now why that might have turned me into public enemy number one to some of the other girls, especially since whenever anyone saw me, I was just so damn excited.

As time went on, though, and I became more established, I noticed a shift in some of the girls' demeanors. They started to realize that I wasn't just in this for a season; I was here to stay. Some of their attitudes adjusted, though others never came back around. Now, though, I understand I also had something that so many of the other girls didn't: protection from the men around me.

While there was internal competition in the Ruff Ryders camp, it wasn't something that made people feel like they were fighting for a seat at the table. We were all seen as equal, even me. They never saw me as "the girl" they could throw on a track for good measure. I was in boot camp with them; I was in the trenches. If they were in the studio for twenty-four hours, then so was I. Twenty-seven hours? I was there too. I didn't need anybody to feel sorry for me or hold my fucking bag for me.

And what was especially respected, was that when it was time to trade our bars, I was ready for war. Friendly competition, but not a catfight. The guys knew that my mindset was like, "Look, I love you, but I'm gonna have to murder you on this track." That's just how it goes. I knew deep down that, yeah, I was the girl—the *only* girl—on these tracks, so I had to go in. I earned respect by showing up, both physically and lyrically. I was one of them,

and when it came time to let me grow, everyone let me
fly while still guiding me along the way. Dee showed me
how to sit and really write my songs and slow down with
my delivery. It wasn't because I was some damsel in distress—he just wanted me to win. The guys in the Ruff
Ryders never hurt me, never disrespected me, and if anyone else tried to, they'd be dealt with. No questions asked.
I felt safe, while so many of the girls around me weren't.
Chivon also showed up to some of my photo and video
shoots, so I wasn't always the only girl in the room. I had
guys like Dee, Waah and Swizz—whose granddad was an
imam and helped build mosques—around me. They didn't
try to enforce Islam over me or anything, but they knew
my relationship with the religion and my proximity to it,
and it was nice to see them practicing it. At the same time,
they weren't going to urge me to talk about sex, and they
weren't going to make me dress sexy. In fact, it was actually
more *me* arguing with *them* about how they had to let me
do my thing. If I was trying to take more clothes off, then
they were definitely trying to cover me up. Waah used to
be like, "Here, put this vest on," or, "Here, put this hoodie
on," and I'd be like, "What? No!" If they had a problem
with a line I wrote or an outfit I had on, I'd check them for
it, but you know what? Better that than having them trying to put me out there looking a certain way that I might
regret. And it was great because I knew they'd always see
me for my lyrics and nothing else. It wasn't really in my
nature to go overboard with all of that other stuff, anyway.
I wanted to be known as the girl who could hang with the
boys yet still be sexy, but I didn't want that sexiness to be
too overt. I also *needed* to be respected lyrically. I hated that
"you're good for a girl" shit. Fuck that. I'm good because

I'm good. The men around me knew that even though I was the First Lady, I was strong enough to hold my own on songs—both with them and without them.

As for the other guys in Ruff Ryders, like X and the Lox and all of them, they guarded me with their lives too. I was their sister. One time, Mike Tyson tried talking to me crazy when I was out with the Lox. The guys saw I was noticeably uncomfortable, and they were about to fight Mike Tyson to protect me. Literally, Styles P, Jadakiss, and Sheek Louch were building a strategy around how they were going to potentially gang up on Iron Mike Tyson. Hell, Styles had a knife on him and was ready to shank Mike in my honor! It was like *that* when it came to respecting me. And even when the core unit of the Ruff Ryders wasn't there to protect me, all of the other Ruff Ryders who rode with them were. Those are the kinds of guys that I had around me. I know for a fact that some of the other girls weren't as lucky, and knowing that I was being positioned to win by the men around me was way different from how some of my peers were dealt with. Mixed with the fact that in my mind, my only real competition was myself, it didn't sit right with some of the girls.

I've learned through the years, just experiencing everything that's happened, that so much of the fighting between women in hip-hop really has nothing to do with us. It's the men behind the women kind of forcing this war. And as Black women in music (and the world), we are coming in with so much trauma from how we're treated and it only makes matters worse. So we fight with each other instead of with the people who actually deserve our rage.

But women passing all of that pent-up anger onto me—and not the men around *them*—was only going to make me wanna work harder. And really, the attitudes and actions from some of the girls ignited something within me. I already had the fire, but the disrespect sparked an inferno. I was like, "Cool, I'm done with trying to be friends. Now I'm gonna show you what I can *really* do." I might have dropped the "Destruction" from my name by then, but I was gonna lyrically destroy anyone who tried to get in my way. You wanna hate me? Now I was gonna give you a reason to.

7

LET THERE BE EVE

I was the first person to hold my friend's baby, after holding her hand as she went through labor. I didn't need science class to show me how a baby was born: I was standing right there in the maternity ward in the early hours of the morning, with my friend propped up in the hospital bed. I was only sixteen years old. She was seventeen, but her boyfriend was much older. He'd left her all alone at the hospital, just as their baby was about to be born. I honestly wasn't shocked, especially since she still had cuts and bruises healing on her face as her child came into the world. After she had her baby, she had to go back to the hospital to get even more stitches—not from the delivery, but for her face again. She used to come over to my house a lot with bruises on her; sometimes her face would just be so swollen, black and blue and banged up from the fists of that man. That *grown*-ass man, who later got her pregnant and left her. I got home from the hospital that day and wrote a poem about it:

I don't even know you and I hate you...
See all I know is that my girlfriend used to date you...

I kept writing more. I had to. I was so mad and needed a place to put it.

Four years later, the first stanza of my poem became the first few lines of "Love Is Blind." She didn't die (thank God), and I didn't shoot her ex dead (thank God for that too), but when I got in the studio, I thought about my friend and how we had to deal with so much shit at that time, and how we were both just kids. While I wrote that song as a twenty-year-old, beyond the lines of my teenage poem, I thought about the what-ifs. What if he beat her to death and her child became an orphan? What if I had him in a corner with a gun in my hand? What if I pulled the trigger? Moved by all of the possible outcomes that (thankfully) never came to be, I wrote that song. The poem was originally a safe space for my feelings in the moment; the song became my therapy, to finally process the trauma of what I saw as a teen. When I recorded "Love Is Blind," the guys were all supportive of it. They respected the song not only for its lyrical content but also the messaging behind it. I didn't expect it to take off like it did.

That song was initially for *me*, but later on, when the rest of the world heard it, I understood it was for *them*. When I went on a talk show, I brought my friend with me so that everyone could hear her story from her own mouth and see that she'd thankfully survived. She was one of the lucky ones. That song was felt on a deeper level—more than I could even comprehend. There are people who still come up to me to this day and tell me how that song has helped them. It's something that I don't take lightly. It's not always our responsibility as artists to change the world, but when you do, it matters. I mean, the fact that a song about domestic violence was the third single on my debut album showed that my team and I had all taken a leap of faith.

And it worked.

The year before my album dropped, X dropped two albums: his debut, *It's Dark and Hell Is Hot* and, *Flesh of My Flesh, Blood of My Blood*. By '99, The Lox were with us, but were still coming out of their Bad Boy situation, where they had dropped their debut, *Money, Power & Respect*. They were getting prepared for their Ruff Ryders debut, *We Are the Streets*, to drop at the start of the following year, so the runway was clear for my album to take off and really be the star of the show, which to me was also a sign of respect. I went from fighting for an album on Aftermath to having the priority album on Ruff Ryders. I was taking it all in, even though everything was moving *so* quickly. I'm talking about photo shoots and studio sessions, writing, writing, writing, while keeping up with the demands of being that "it" girl who everyone wanted to hear. It was a constant, nonstop cycle—from getting up to working in the studio and drinking, smoking weed, then back at it. The momentum was strong and the anticipation for what I had coming next was really the focus. I trusted the process, but I also trusted who I had around me, so this was a time when I wasn't hanging out in all of the business meetings. I kept it strictly to the music and whatever was needed to push that music. I was enjoying the ride.

Those "boot camp" writing sessions when I first joined the Ruff Ryders really helped me with everything—from my songwriting speed to song structure—so by the time my debut album came around, I was like a conditioned athlete. I kind of had to be. After the response to my verse on the remix to "Ruff Ryder's Anthem," it was basically decided within like three days that I had to get to work on *Let There Be Eve... Ruff Ryders' First Lady*.

I was primed for it, but I had my coach (Dee) working with me. For a former street dude, his creativity was crazy. I don't know if he'd always had musical aspirations, but man, he just knew how to help me execute my vision and make me the best emcee I could be. Coming from Philly, we just talk really fast, and that carried over into my early rhymes (you can hear it on that first remix), but Dee taught me how to slow down. I still came in with the spirit of a battle rapper, like, "I got sixteen bars! I got twenty-four! Forty-eight! Bars, bars, bars!" Dee would be like, "Okay, that's cool, but let's figure out how to make this eight. Or twelve? We have to get back to the chorus." He showed me how to make actual songs. He also knew *how* to offer suggestions, where it didn't feel like I was being forced to alter my shit. I always felt like it was for my greater development, and he *never* tried to police the content I put in.

It was just natural for me to not talk about sex or my body in like every bar. It just never was my thing. I think that part of me did come from being in a cypher as a battle rapper, because you can't really talk about that kind of stuff there. The goal was to take the other person down, plain and simple. I'm not gonna take anyone down with "pussy, pussy, pussy" bars; if anything, that'd be more fuel to help take *me* down. I was obsessed with upholding my lyrical content, while trying to emulate some of my heroes on the mic, like Black Thought and Lauryn Hill. My pussy didn't need to enter the conversation like that.

Production-wise, the bulk of that album came from Swizz Beatz, who was also way on the come-up since he was the one who'd produced "Ruff Ryder's Anthem." Swizz and I grew side by side in that camp. Despite being the nephew of the owners, Swizz didn't benefit from *any* nepotism whatsoever. In fact, he had to work *harder* to establish himself because Dee and Waah refused to just hand it to him. But it was great, and we just naturally became like brother and sister. Since we were the same age and going through similar growth spurts in this game, I loved having him there and getting to work with him. We were in the same space, because he had to prove he wasn't just a family member getting in through the bloodline and I had to prove I wasn't just the token girl with the obvious visibility. This was never really discussed between us, but it was so apparent in the way we worked. And Swizz is just *so quick*. It's incredible, and it made working and writing with him just so easy. He helped me work quicker as well. He's still one of the easiest producers I've worked with, and something that I think is a lost art is how a producer is supposed to *produce* you and not just make a beat and hand it to you. Swizz Beatz is a *real producer*. Period.

The album flowed pretty fast, because after we'd finished one song, Swizz would say, "I've got another beat ready," and I'd be like, "All right, well, let's go!" I had *no* shortage of words and Swizz had *no* shortage of beats.

"What Y'all Want" was technically my first single, even though it was on the Ruff Ryders compilation. We put a remix of it on my album, but the first song to be heard on its own after that compilation project was "Gotta Man." I sang the hook on that one too, but we later put Mashonda on it and had her sing the hook as well. My late A&R Icepick's daughter is the little girl who says, "I gotta boyfriend now" at the beginning. The irony of "Gotta Man" is that Swizz played it for another rapper after we got Mashonda on the hook, and he was basically like, "I want a song like this." He didn't just want the beat, either. He wanted the *whole* thing: the light, airy beat, but also the playful singing on the hook. Hell, he even wanted *Mashonda* on the hook, and that's what he got when he got *his* version of the song. The song was even released before "Gotta Man"; he didn't let that sit in the vault for very long. That didn't bother me at all, honestly. If anything, it just reaffirmed what I knew and had wanted the whole time: that *men* saw me as their competition even more than women. Mission accomplished.

The funniest memory I have from creating that song, though, is from the music video. We had Mashonda in it, but at the time, she was signed to the "Madd Rapper" Deric "D-Dot" Angelettie, and after she did the video, I think he tried to charge us what seemed like an outrageous amount of money to have her in it. We weren't gonna accept *that*, but what my guys tried to do instead was even worse: they attempted to just put a black spot where Mashonda's face was in the video. It was just so janky and hilarious, like in some random scene you'd see a black spot floating by. I don't think that version of the video even saw the light of day, but it existed at one point. The final video has those shots clipped out entirely.

Selecting that song as the single was a group effort, since once I had my songs done, everyone just sat and listened to them over and over and over. Dee was mainly in charge of that, along with Icepick, who A&R'd the project. We had outside people come through to the studio and listen too. They were definitely playing chess with everything; there was no throwing shit against the wall to see what stuck. It was assessing all of the moves we were making and ensuring that everything I did made sense. It was all very structured, while content-wise they just let me be me and listened to my vision for the rollout, especially the music videos. Like, for "Love Is Blind," I really wanted the visuals to be cinematic but intense. We eventually got Faith Evans on the remix once it became a single, and she appeared in the video too. The video's director, Dave Meyers, really heard me on that. Benny Boom was actually the assistant director on that video (he even has a walk-on scene), and years later, when we were working together on the TV show *Queens*, we talked about that whole experience. It was a gamble, but everyone had been behind me on it. The fact that Dave Meyers later won a Grammy and other awards for his music video work and Benny Boom became not only a famous music video director but a director for TV and film is amazing, since I had them working with me at the very start of my career.

It only took two months to make my debut album, which is crazy in and of itself. There are so many people who were a part of that album—people who were a part of my life back then, and a part of the journey leading up to the project. Girls who I used to hang out with were on some skits and on some of the hooks. I had homies from Philly who would come up to New York to hang out with me. I consider my first album to be my "Philly album," even though I recorded most of it in Midtown Manhattan at the STU, where every rapper was recording their music; now I was there too.

I feel like I waited my entire life to write my debut album, which is why so much of it felt like I was just pouring my heart out all over the music. I was fueled up and ready to go, to say the least. I knew what I wanted, what I wanted to talk about and how I wanted it to sound. I also wanted to do some singing on some of the songs' hooks ("Love Is Blind" being one of them). The guys never even questioned it, really. It was something I wanted to try, and they were cool with it. They were cool with all of it. The music was my outlet. I still reserved *some* vulnerability in the songwriting—that's the Scorpio in me—but I just had so much to say and had never had eighteen tracks before to do it. It was my life, set to music. You could hear it on songs that like "Heaven Only Knows," where I really wanted people to understand who I was as a person and the things that I had been through before I stepped into the spotlight. I got to Philly the fuck out with Beanie Sigel on "Philly, Philly." I got to work with one of the few girls who I actually called my friend, Missy Elliott, on "Ain't Got No Dough," but most of all I had the Ruff Ryders with me all over the album. We had Swizz on the beats; I had X on some songs, Drag-On, the Lox. My family—from my Philly life to my New York City one—were all there and a part of the project. It felt good.

On September 14, 1999, my very first album, *Let There Be Eve… Ruff Ryders' First Lady,* was released. It's hard to explain what that felt like, mainly because, again, it just happened *so* fast. I didn't have any time to process what was happening, and before I knew it, I was selling like two hundred thousand copies in the first week alone—not to mention hitting the number one spot on the Billboard 200, as the third rap girl ever to do that after Lauryn Hill and Foxy Brown. *Surreal* is not even the word. It was a whirlwind after that.

I remember, though, the moment that I really felt like I had *made it* was standing on the set of Missy Elliott's music video for the "Hot Boyz" remix. When I wrote my verse,

I knew I'd be alongside heavy hitters like Nas and Q-Tip on the track, along with Missy, obviously. I wanted to make sure I did my thing and stood out. It's still one of my favorite verses to perform to this day, but the video is something I will never forget. That was my first time standing on the set of a Hype Williams music video. It felt like money, extravagance, you name it... This was at a time when they were *really* giving out huge budgets for music videos. I stood there in my fur vest in a gigantic space and looked around in shock. I can still see that set so vividly, with its big, big metal fixtures and flashing lights. I thought to myself, "There's a *crane*? There's *fire*? There's *Nas*? There's *Missy*?" It was such a vibe, but more importantly, I saw it as this new level that I was on. Like, "What? I'm a part of *this*? This is *definitely* making it." Because I was on this huge video set, where Hype Williams was getting like a million dollars for a *video*! And it was *Hyper*. All of it. Everything was intense. I was such a newbie, but I also felt deep inside that this was where I belonged.

My name was everywhere; I was everywhere. I was being invited to places I had never been before. I'm talking about flying to Jamaica (which quickly became one of my favorite places in the world) to film the Bob Marley TV Special *One Love: The Bob Marley All-Star Tribute* alongside Lauryn Hill, Queen Latifah and Erykah Badu, among so many other legends. I even got to perform *with* a Marley. Stephen and I performed Bob's song "Rat Race." It was an absolutely crazy experience, but some changes were happening during my whole album rollout too.

I felt like my manager, Marc, was becoming less and less available. His cousin Troy Carter was around a lot more. Ironically, I knew Troy from when I was like fifteen trying to audition for him, and here he was now, helping me along my journey. Eventually, I fired Marc and hired Troy. There were no hard feelings, but things were just moving too quickly and I needed the support.

One day Troy called me and told me that Prince wanted to do a song with me. I was like, "Get the fuck out of here. That's a lie." It wasn't. Prince was coming to New York, and I was told that when I got the call, I had to drop everything and head right to the studio. That was *not* a hard sacrifice to make. Like a month went by, and then Troy finally called to tell me to head to the studio. I said to myself, "Fuck. I'm gonna meet Prince!" I got to Electric Lady, and he wasn't there. I really thought Troy was pranking me (he did that sometimes) until Prince walked in with his then-wife Mayte. My first thought was, "How is this man so pretty?" He said to me, "I really like your music. 'What Y'all Want' is a cool record." I did *not* know what to do with myself. He wanted me to add a verse to his song "The Greatest Romance Ever Sold" as an "Adam and Eve" remix. He was going to go see Lenny Kravitz at a concert and was like, "I'll see you when I get back." He didn't even make it to that concert before I already had my verse done. I was just so excited. When he got back (with Lenny Kravitz no less!) I had my verse ready. Prince was shocked. I was shocked he knew who the fuck I was, so I guess we were even. It was not even two years ago that I had been on this roller coaster ride of feeling hopeful and then hopeless, and now I was the "it" girl in hip-hop, getting invited to fashion shows and showing up on songs with Prince.

They say that your new life is gonna cost you your old one, though, and I didn't know just how real that was going to get...

...until I went on tour.

8

LOVE IS (REALLY) BLIND

I am curled up in the fetal position on the bathroom floor of my hotel room. Sobbing uncontrollably. I couldn't stop, but I also couldn't breathe. I tried to calm down, but it was as if I was on total autopilot. My body was telling me that I was in a state of emergency, yet I couldn't get up to run. Where would I run to anyway? Where was I going? My heart was racing, almost as fast as my breath, and the tears just kept flowing and flowing. I called my manager, Troy. He heard me being suffocated by my own emotions and came running to my room. As he got down on the floor with me, all he said was, "Let's pray."

I didn't know what anxiety was, exactly, but I knew that what I had just experienced was nothing short of terrifying. Something also told me that it wasn't just a momentary feeling of terror. It was a buildup of my emotions, really, that finally exploded. Here I was on the Ruff Ryders/Cash Money

Tour at the start of 2000, and we were supposed to hit thirty different stops in two months' time. Meanwhile, I was being pulled in every possible direction. I had just turned twenty-one, and I was thrust into a life I had never known before. Sure, it was the life I claimed I'd always wanted, but once you're in the thick of it, it's harder to see all of the good—the bad keeps popping out at you. I craved familiarity on this new ride, so I brought some of my friends from Philly along with me. Here's the thing about fame: your life gets weirder once the people around you start getting weird. The energies shift, and no one knows how to handle it. The reality is *everyone* in that orbit changes, both the people experiencing the fame and then those around them. I didn't believe that was a real phenomenon that could happen to me and the people around me until it was staring me right in the face. In my case, it was the constant reminders from my friends that I was the one changing, as I was so stubborn about showing them that I was the same old Eve from West Philadelphia who could party until the sun came up. I think I knew that wasn't true, but then you start feeling guilty about that, and so you try even harder. Meanwhile, I'm here having to navigate and adjust to this new life while they seemed pretty content in their ways. No judgment, but I had work to do. I had to be onstage every day; I had to be accountable *and* be a professional. *Professional.* I had to learn what that word *really* meant, the hard way.

I brought three friends along with me on that tour—two girls and one guy. I gave them all jobs, which they never did, but I wanted them to have money in their pockets. One friend was assigned wardrobe duty. And I don't mean she had to style me or anything. Her one job was just to bring my outfits to each venue on the tour. That didn't happen. I had my little cousins come along and help me, and I even had to start doing some of the work myself while still showing up every night onstage. I was trapped in a hurricane of my own making. Then there was all the partying. Everyone was smoking weed and drinking, and I wanted to keep up with them still, so I kept doing it too. I was always tired and I had vocal fry like I was a seventy-five-year-old chain smoker. It became a vicious cycle of drinking, smoking weed, doing my friends' jobs, getting back onstage, then drinking and smoking some more.

Troy used to refuse to come on my tour bus to have conversations with me. If he needed to talk to me, he'd make me get off the bus and come talk to him outside. "I don't like the energy on the bus," he'd tell me. "It feels like the devil is on there." The Philly in me always barked back at him like, "Don't be talking about my friends like that!" I wouldn't call my friends devils, but there were a lot of demons being fought on that bus. My two girls started fighting with each other, because one was being paid a little more. The girl math in my head rationalized that because the one girl had a daughter, so I figured she could use a little more in her check. My other friend disagreed and a fight ensued. Then my guy friend just checked out and hung out more and more with the Ruff Ryders crew. That annoyed me. I then had my *other* guy friend from LA come on tour (since I didn't have enough chaos already) and he wound up having a "situation" with my assistant. Meanwhile, one of my girls decided that she should be my hype girl and hopped onstage looking crazy. Her makeup was so piled on that she looked like a clown, which didn't match my vibe at all. We got into an argument right after.

Once they started noticing my frustration, that's when

the Hunger Games really started between them. My friends would try to take each other down to see who could stay on and make the most money and who could be bumped out of the race. They'd snitch on each other to me like, "Yo, so and so has your bracelet!" It was just all so ridiculous. Even with all of that going on, the Ruff Ryders let me do my thing, until Dee had to pull me to the side and be like, "You're the artist here. This can't keep happening." It was a real lesson for me, and the first one I had to learn about the other people on your journey. Not everybody's supposed to be there—and no matter what you do, no matter how much you try to set them up for success, not everyone can come along with you. When Lauryn Hill said, "It's funny how money change a situation," she wasn't kidding. I was living through it, and I had no clue how to balance things. Loyalty and logic can be best friends—or they can be mortal enemies.

It all came to a head when we reached New York. During the tour, I had to film the music video for Beanie Sigel's song "Remember Them Days," which I was featured on. When I got back to my hotel room after the shoot, I had finally reached my limit. I walked into the bathroom, closed the door and locked it. Then I started screaming the loudest that I've ever screamed in my entire life. My assistant was in the hotel room with me when she heard the screams bleeding through the bathroom door. I started bawling and couldn't stop. I couldn't even recognize myself. My crying, my screams—I didn't even know the sound of my own voice. *Who is this?* I thought. But it was me, and I couldn't get myself under control. My assistant tried to get into the bathroom, but I couldn't even make a move to unlock the door, so she kicked the door down. There

I was on the floor, emotionally in a million little pieces. I looked up at her and said, "I'm just not happy. I'm just so sad. I can't do this tour anymore." There were only a few days left, but I didn't have it in me. I was depleted.

When Troy got to the hotel room and we started praying, he told me that I could probably leave the tour without being sued since there were only a few days left. "I'll do what I can," he said. "But you're just broken. You are *completely* broken." He didn't fight me on wanting to leave, especially after seeing me in that condition. There was no way that I could finish. I *was* able to leave the tour, thankfully. There was really no other option. I had experienced a nervous breakdown, and so I spent the next six months trying to recover from it—all while keeping my career going as best as I could. I knew that I had to make some real changes for myself.

For starters, I had to wean myself off drinking and smoking weed before I entered any situation involving my music. That was trial and error for me, but I learned that it really came down to how I wanted to be as a performer. I would see all of these rap dudes just high as fuck onstage, and I'd wonder how it'd all worked out for them. Honestly, it kind of hadn't, since so many of them bored me because they weren't connecting with their audience. They can be high on drugs or ego, but whatever it is, there's an empty connection happening.

I think that's what drew me to the theatrical aspect of battle rap: how you have to be so exaggerated and bold with your body and your words to elicit a response from a crowd. The same goes for traditional concert performances, at least in my eyes. When I step onstage, my goal is to raise the vibration of every person in that room, and that can't happen if my mind isn't clear. I don't go to church, so the stage is my church, and if I can't show up to church in the best way possible, then I don't do it. That goes for the wardrobe, the stage setup, the graphics, the dancers, me and my mindset. I have turned down opportunities if the vibe is off. It might sound crazy, but it's something I've had to stand behind throughout my entire career. When I was spiraling, I canceled those last few tour dates too because I couldn't give the crowd my all. The audience is there to have a good time, and it's my job to provide it. The same goes for the studio. Much like the stage, it's a sacred space to me, and if I take one sip of liquor in that room, then I'd better be done recording the music. Otherwise, it goes from a recording session to a listening session. I keep up these practices to this day, but they first started during that tour, when I had to clean house, both mentally and physically. A lot of ties had to be severed during that time. I fired everyone I had with me, except for Troy. That's when he became my formal manager. But most of all, I had to sever ties with my old self in exchange for my new self. It had to be done.

There was just one other breakup that I had to go through with, but that one took a little longer...

He was older than me, and he was already seasoned in the music industry. And I thought I was in love. I'd had high school boyfriends and whatever before then, but I never took them seriously. This was my first *real* and *serious* relationship, and it started while I was in the eye of the storm at the start of my career. He chased me, though, and somehow he gradually won me over. The Ruff Ryders all hated him, but his presence became more and more frequent. We kept bumping into each other at the studio or at industry events, wherever and whenever. We were both in New York, so it was nothing to both be in the same place recording or at the same party. The industry is so incestuous in that way. I ignored every red flag with him—from other girls in his bed when we first started dating to other girls in our bed while we were in a serious relationship. Troy tried to keep him off my tour bus and wouldn't let him into the studio, even though he'd keep trying to get in. "He's not coming into this studio," Troy would tell me. When I was in the studio with Prince, he was damn near going to charter a helicopter to Electric Lady. "But I *have to* be there!"

During those six months following my breakdown, I was miserable for a number of reasons. I was being cheated on and lied to daily, constantly fighting, all while I still had to "show up" as part of a couple with him in the public eye. I was noticeably annoyed on red carpets, and I was slowly checking out. My mental health was hanging on by a thread because all of the other stuff that was going on, and this was the added drama I didn't need. We would be out to dinner at a restaurant, and out of nowhere I would just start crying. Like, I couldn't even control my emotions, which was definitely something that I wasn't used to. It got to the point where I didn't want to be anywhere, while he wanted to be everywhere. I'd like to think we both knew it wasn't a good fit, but that's just how codependency works in a toxic relationship. I let it linger on during my "recovery" period. We were living together, so I kind of had no choice. I eventually moved out and bought a house far out in New Jersey, near upstate New York. We still kept going, even once we weren't under the same roof, though my strength started slowly coming back. One thing was for certain: I knew it was over in my heart.

The Ruff Ryders ended up renting a house in Miami to

record our next projects, so I moved down there with them for two months. He followed, but I was already checked out, and just happy to be back around my brothers. I had my Yorkie Spunky with me, and then I bought Spunky a little friend while I was in Florida, my little Yorkie Bear. So I had my *dawgs* and my *dogs* with me, plus the man who was acting like a *dog* behind my back. What a situation. But for the most part, I loved being in Miami, because I was back in my recording bag and things just started evolving in my songwriting. It became my escape, but also the place where I set my intentions.

Since I was kid, I've always had a vivid imagination, and I would speak things into existence. Once when I was like eight or nine years old, I said to my mother, "Mom, I love you and I love Grandma, but I don't want a regular life. I want something different." At the time, I didn't even know what those words meant to me. I was just a child, and since I never kept a diary back then, I would talk about these dreams out loud. Eventually, they found their way into my notebook, which transferred into my music. When you're coming out of your lowest point, the only thing you can do is visualize your rise back up. At least, that's what I did. Once I got my life story out on my debut, I spent a lot of time writing rhymes about what I was manifesting for myself. It wasn't about the fight or the forcing my way into rooms, it was about putting down on paper the kind of life that I wanted to live. One of my favorite verses I've ever written was on the remix to Jadakiss's "We Gonna Make It" with Styles P. I didn't write about what I had; I wrote about what I planned to have:

I need some private jets / fly to islands to watch the sun set...
A country ranch with thoroughbreds as pets...

I wrote that verse during my time out in Miami with the guys at the Hit Factory recording studio (the hottest spot where all of the rappers recorded), and I had just dyed my hair red but hadn't unveiled it yet. So in the music video, you can see me with a silk scarf on my head, but my red eyebrows are telling on me. That brief time period was an important shift in my consciousness, because that's when I had to return to the little girl explaining to her mom why she was destined for bigger things. I knew the kind of life that I wanted to live and the lifestyle that I wanted to lead, but I had to kiss my old life goodbye for good. The music had to reflect that, but honestly, I knew in my heart that was the goal all along. When I was signed to Aftermath, I was in one of my very few studio sessions with this guy and we wrote this song together. The hook went something like, "Scared money don't make money / I got courage, I take money." The whole song was about being a stick-up chick. It was a dope-ass record, but I didn't use it, because it wasn't me or my personality. Did I know stick-up chicks? Oh, absolutely. I had friends who did that kind of stuff, but it wasn't me, and it wasn't my vibe. I didn't need to rob anybody, not when I had the skills to make the money myself. I always like to believe that I follow my heart, and as I was coming back into my own after six months of total devastation, I had to follow my heart again.

As for my relationship? Well, it ended before *Scorpion* was released. I actually broke up with him through writing my song "You Had Me, You Lost Me," but he didn't know that until the song came out. Whoops. The ripple effect of that relationship, though, haunted me for years and affected how I moved with men in my life after that. I wasn't after love, so I simply started thinking like a man. It took me a really long time to divorce myself from that mentality, even after I was long done with the relationship that caused it. And even though that part of my life is in the rearview mirror, it has still managed to pop up unannounced over the years to haunt me. The only difference is now I'm well equipped to handle it.

9

SCORPION

My mother never got to see me graduate from high school. She didn't get to watch me walk down the aisle and up onto the stage to grab my diploma and shake my principal's hand. She never saw me turn the tassel on my cap from one side to the other, or dramatically throw my cap up into the air like they did in '80s movies. All because I had to go and flunk gym class. Sure, I got my diploma after summer school, but my walking at graduation in my cap and gown would have been a moment for my mom, and she never got it. Graduation wasn't supposed to be for me anyway; it was supposed to be for my mom. Isn't that the point of it all—to show your parents you did it and make them proud? The fact that I robbed my mother of that moment over *gym* class—when she was so supportive of my music career—ate me up for years. I carried that guilt until February 27, 2002, at the 44th Annual Grammy

Awards. I brought my mom with me as my date, and no one else came with us. This was her moment. This was my graduation. I was nominated for two Grammys that year: Best Rap Album for *Scorpion* and Best Rap/Sung Collaboration for "Let Me Blow Ya Mind" with Gwen Stefani.

When they announced my name as the winner for Best Rap/Sung Collaboration, I couldn't believe it. I made history with the Recording Academy as the first winner of that award, since it was a brand-new category. And as I walked up to get my Grammy, my mother watched me do it. *That* was my graduation walk, for *her*. Plus, I had my own Grammy now, with my name on it. That was by far the greatest moment during my *Scorpion* rollout.

It had been nearly two years since *Let There Be Eve... Ruff Ryders' First Lady* dropped, which in hip-hop time was forever. I was already one nervous breakdown in, one public breakup out, plus my profile was growing with magazine covers, performances, fashion shows and song features, so I was a little busy to say the least. But the people wanted music, and by "the people" I mean my record label. It was a lot to pile on me at once, but I guess that's how supply and demand works, right? I call *Scorpion* my "industry" album because that's exactly how it felt to make it. When you're a star on the rise, there's this added pressure to keep delivering and delivering, especially when your debut album hits as hard as mine did. That's when the "sophomore curse" talk starts pouring in, which only adds to the overall urgency to make good music and prove the haters wrong. I was like, "Look, I'm just trying not to end back up crying on a hotel bathroom floor, okay?" But this industry can be merciless, and it's no wonder so many artists (especially Black women) find themselves unable to handle it all. It's because we are the ones mainly thrown out there without a life vest. Many, many times, I've felt like I was left out at sea in my career, but the waves first started crashing over me right around the time *Scorpion* was set to release. In the beginning with my debut album, I took a back seat in all of the business meetings. I was so focused on making the music, since my very first deal with Aftermath had me playing the waiting game. So I just voluntarily let decisions be made for me with Ruff Ryders, and it worked out well for the most part. I mean, there was no real money at that point, and I hadn't even proven myself as an artist yet. But once you're there holding your platinum plaques, you start wondering what's going on in those boardrooms and wanting to chime in; meanwhile, all of the men at the labels preferred you had kept it the other way.

In some ways, my second album was forced upon me. A part of me really believed that after one album I was done. Like, "Okay, I did it! It was number one! Time to move onto the next thing I wanna do!" It doesn't work like that—not when you are successful with the music you make. Before I knew it, the label was telling me that I was pressed for time, and I only had a certain "window" to release my second album. Now there were "windows," when so much of the start of my career at Interscope was spent waiting and me wanting to jump out of one. The irony. In my heart I did want to make more music, and I was excited to do that, but I was just coming out of so much exhaustion in my life and my career. I wanted to take a breather, but they kept pushing me to make this album happen, and fast. I wanted to sit and be creative and think of new things to do with my music. If I had to make another album, couldn't I experiment a little bit? Isn't the point of making music to evolve? Apparently it wasn't then, and so many of my suggestions were met with pushback. I opted to have no theme to the album at all—no rhyme or reason. It's not like every rapper had some themed project, but with my first album, there was a very specific story being told. I was the girl from Philly just getting warmed up and that album was the journey of how I got there. *Scorpion* had more of a "wait and see what I come up with" vibe. I decided to just go in there and hear some beats and write off the vibes and let whatever happened, happen. It was the best (and easiest) way to stay present without overthinking the whole process.

There was also a shift happening on the business side of things. While I was still very much a Ruff Ryder, I had always kept my management separate, and so by the second album, I was more directly an "Interscope" artist now. They were in the driver's seat this time, not the Ruff Ryders. That meant going into these meetings with just Troy and me (and often Icepick, who was also an executive producer with the Ruff Ryders), and not really having the Dee and Waah combo that I had when I was making my first album. Of course, they were still there creatively, but all of this business stuff was really me going in without them. That was an adjustment too. Sitting in those meetings for what honestly was the first time, I started to see firsthand how I wasn't being heard. It's a different story when the messages are being delivered to you in a studio booth and the guys are the ones handling the negotiations. I probably wasn't as big of an investment back then either, until lightning struck with *Let There Be Eve*. Now I'm here, the artist with the proven hits, trying to express my vision and getting a lot of blank faces in return. My ideas weren't so far out there, either, and we later saw how well they worked. A while after *Scorpion* dropped, Icepick called me out of the blue and apologized. He said to me, "I just want to apologize to you because I think sometimes we should have listened to you more about the suggestions you had." That meant a lot to me and validated that I wasn't crazy in my ideas. It was just that the wrong people were hearing them, or maybe they didn't expect—or *respect*—the person who was providing them. They did listen to one of my ideas, and that was to get Gwen Stefani on "Let Me Blow Ya Mind," but even *that* was an uphill battle.

Before "Let Me Blow Ya Mind" was in the works, Interscope came up with their big plan: they wanted me back in the studio with Dr. Dre. Now, in my head, he was like my archnemesis, the dude who I'd thought was going to give me my big break but instead handed it over to the other bleached blonde rapper. I was so annoyed and at first didn't want to work with Dre at all. Jimmy Iovine insisted though, and it's like, how do you tell the big boss "no"? But since Scott Storch was also producing on the record, and he used to let me sneak into the studio back in Philly at like fifteen to write songs, I rationalized that our collaboration would be a "Philly" thing. I had to do whatever it took to make me okay with working with Dre, and it began with "Let Me Blow Ya Mind."

Reuniting with Dre was messy. I mean, can I even call it a reunion, when this was really the first time he was actually fucking with me and not sending someone else in his place? I entered into this process with a whole lot of resentment toward him. When we hit the studio, I was like a remixed version of my Philly self. Yes, he was the star producer, but I was the star rapper. *Nobody* wanted to be in the studio with us. We would yell at each other and exchange more fuck-yous than actual directions on the music. The thing about Dre, though, is he brings something out of you. He *makes* you wanna show up even harder. And as much as he pissed me off, he brought out the best in me when I made songs. I wrote "Let Me Blow Ya Mind" from start to finish all by myself, hook and all. And yeah, I threw a few shots at a couple of the girls on that song (contrary to popular belief, it wasn't one girl in particular), but if I was going to do this, then I was going all-in.

Once I had the hook written (I sing on parts of that too), there was only one person that I wanted on it: Gwen Stefani. She was literally the first person who came to mind. I was a huge No Doubt fan, and it just felt like the perfect mash-up. As different as we were, we were also both "just a girl" in a group of dudes, so I related to her. Pretty much everyone at the label pushed back on that. It got to the point where I was like, "Look, Gwen is the *only* person I want on this hook, so if it's not her then I'll just do it myself." It wasn't like it was Jimmy or even Dre who was pushing back at me—it was more so everyone else on the label side. They were saying things like, "No one is going to believe this," (I still don't even know what that means) and then asking, "Well, how do we categorize this? Is it hip-hop?" No imagination whatsoever. I tried showing them past examples of similar collaborations. I said, "What about Run-DMC and Aerosmith? They did 'Walk This Way' together and it worked. We have proof that it can work. It has happened before and it was successful." They didn't wanna hear me. I basically had to beg them to let me do this, and my rationale was like, "Look, she's signed to Interscope too, so that part is easy, and she might even say no, but can we just try?" They finally agreed, and when they asked Gwen Stefani, she immediately said yes. We got on the phone, and I told Gwen she can change up whatever lyrics she wanted to on the hook out of respect, since she's a songwriter too. She was like, "No, I think this is perfect! I'll just sing what's here." The first time we met in person was when we filmed the music video. The result of that collaboration was not only a Grammy but another song together, "Rich Girl," on Gwen's album *Love. Angel. Music. Baby.* like three years later. And I made a friend in the process, who I still get to perform with to this day. I remember that same year "Let Me Blow Ya Mind" dropped, we walked the BET Awards Red Carpet together, which was a first. You had the First Lady of the Ruff Ryders and the First Lady of No Doubt, walking in there side by side. That made some headlines, and we loved it.

As for Dre, we kept working together. He also produced "That's What It Is" off the album, and we even made more music together when I moved over to *Eve-Olution*, like my single "Satisfaction." I did *not* make his time in the studio with me easy, though, as my quiet redemption. They used to call me the Queen of Nah, because he would come with a beat and I'd be like, "Nah…" That was my own way of getting back at him like, "Fuck you, Dr. Dre! That beat ain't hot!" Dre's a genius, though, and some of my best songs are with him on the production, so there was definitely a love/hate thing going on there.

Even with this being the "industry" album, it helped me in some ways I didn't expect. When I finished "You Had Me, You Lost Me," I had actually come to the point where I was mentally done with my romantic relationship and ready to move on. That song was like the final act for me. Music was the place to put my emotions, almost like a diary sometimes. I needed that place to put my feelings; this whole process was way different from the last. I didn't have my old friends with me anymore—so many of them were gone by then.

My cousin would be there sometimes, and sometimes other family members. But really it was just me, which I think also played into my feelings about it being an "industry" album. It was me, the artist, but in a big expensive studio with label execs now coming in and out. It was so… corporate. My first album was way more organic. I had people around me that I actually knew. Now it was like eight different people from the label popping in to show they were doing their jobs (whatever they were) and asking me if I needed anything. I needed to make *an album*, since everyone was pressuring me.

I did get to do some cool things with *Scorpion* though, like getting the legendary R&B singer Teena Marie on "Life Is So Hard." I *loved* her and was such a fan, so having her be a part of such an emotional song for me really added to the vibe of the project. I got to work with the Marley brothers on "No, No, No," which was so dope as a Bob Marley fan, but also because I got to work with Stephen again after the tribute, and now Damian too. I got to work with more girls like Trina and Da Brat on "Gangsta Bitches," which I loved. I still had my Ruff Ryders with me, and I even did more skits like I had on the first album, even though most of my friends weren't there.

My single "Who's That Girl?" *felt* like a hit, but I didn't really expect it to keep popping up everywhere, even years and years later. I consider that my first real "pop" song, and it was an unpredictable one. We didn't go in with any expectations that it would be "the one" or even "one of the ones," and I don't think anyone knew that it was going to blow up like it did. With *Scorpion*, we definitely kept to the tradition from my first album, where we played the songs over and over and over again until we found our favorites. And "Who's That Girl?" definitely stuck out, especially with the heavy horns that the producer Teflon put on the beat. But the song being on a Top 40 level, to the point where even now I'm contacted like twice a month about placements for it in commercials, movies and TV shows? No, that was not predicted by anyone in the room, especially not by me.

When we were doing the video for "Who's That Girl?" it was Dee and Waah who were like, "We have to get the Harlem Shakers in there. That's what the hood is doing. We gotta put it in there, and we gotta get these kids. Everybody's gonna fuckin' love it." So we got the kids from Harlem who actually started the dance and had them in the music video. It was a nice contrast to all of the "industry" stuff happening. But another shift was in my fashion sense. I had started working with Kithe Brewster as my stylist, and he really introduced me to the fashion world. He got me into the shows and things like that. So in the "Who's That Girl?" video, I'm wearing Chanel and Roberto Cavalli. It was a big difference from getting dressed in the back of a car for my first music video. Only like two or three years earlier, I had never even been on a plane before either, and then I was traveling to places like Japan to perform my songs. The space of time between being just a "regular person" and a "star" was still so short, so at that point on the ride, my old life was not that far in the rearview mirror.

I titled the album *Scorpion* as a nod to my Scorpio sign (sun and rising), and in astrology the color associated with

Scorpio is red. I was obsessed with the red theme after that—that's why I dyed my hair red (though it then broke off) and all of the album art was red-themed. The promo was red-themed. Everything had to be red. That part came together perfectly. I do wish I'd had more time to make the album, though. I only had about two months to put it together. There were days where I felt so rushed: I'd be sitting in the studio in these back-to-back writing sessions (which I hated doing) and just wondering what I was doing there. I didn't have time to really sit with my music—maybe not as long as the first album, since that was like two decades of feelings put into words. But I didn't have time to let anything marinate before it was onto the next song. That was not a process that I was used to, so it was another level I was hitting, where it was new scenery with a new cast of characters and responsibilities. But you adjust; you have no choice. My only regret with that project is that I wish I had taken in the process more instead of feeling like I was making it with a gun to my back. Still, though, we got some *amazing* records out of it, and it was really the closing of yet another chapter in my life.

When *Scorpion* finally released, though, the questions came: "Can she sustain this success? Can lightning strike twice? Are there going to be hits on this record?" The magnifying glass was on me and my music. And as I left that rollout with a Grammy in one hand and a platinum plaque in the other, I guess the answer to all of those questions was "yes."

10

EVE-OLUTION

After *Scorpion*, I was still seeing red, so what did I do? I called in a Blood.

I honestly didn't see what the big deal was with Suge Knight. I mean, I guess I *kind* of got it, based on his whole Death Row reputation. He was like the big, scary, violent bully in hip-hop. Everybody knew who he was, and you didn't really have to know anything about rap to know about Suge Knight. If anyone looked up his name, they'd see he was connected to some terrible shit that existed in hip-hop at the time. He was the dude people avoided, and for that reason, he felt like the perfect person for me to approach to shake down my record label.

Okay, wait, let me explain…

Scorpion had released in the spring of 2001, and by the summer I was heading into my label renegotiations. If we were about to jump into money talks, then I was in a *prime* position to get this talk going. *Let There Be Eve* was double platinum, *Scorpion* was already platinum, it was in the top five on the Billboard 200, I had singles on Top 40 radio (which was major for a rapper), and we learned within a few months that *Scorpion* was nominated for two Grammys (I'd later win one of them). As much as I kept saying the process with *Scorpion* was so "industry," I was now in the pop world. And that was huge for a female rapper. I was also in the fashion world and heading into the film world. I was a star in every sense of the word, and Interscope knew it. I mean, I had even collaborated with Michael Jackson on the remix to his "Butterflies" song. *Michael. Jackson.* The irony of that situation was that I never actually got to meet Michael. He was having some issues with his label, so the music video with us never happened. I'd received a rough treatment for it, where I was supposed to be in some shots in a convertible with Michael Jackson himself! Didn't get to happen. Cut to a few years later, when I'm out in Beverly Hills and heading to the gym one day, and this big black SUV is blocking traffic outside of a medical center right near my gym's entrance. I start beeping my horn as a giant security guy kind of waves his hand at me to calm me down, and the SUV door swings open. I see the white sock and the black loafer step down. Who was it? Michael Jackson. He was in a surgical mask and he waved at me to thank me. I'm sure it all happened so quick that he had *no* idea who I was. I think I blacked out after that and *somehow* made it to my gym. When I got there, my trainer Michelle was like, "What's wrong?!" I said, "Yo, I just saw Michael Jackson." Michelle was also a friend of mine and knew how badly I wanted to meet Michael. She said to me, "Bitch! Fuck this session! Let's *go!*" I told her no, and that

I would get to meet him one day because he was working with Swizz. Two weeks later, Michael Jackson passed away. I later found out from a friend who was at the medical center that day that Michael was so kind, was greeting fans and talking with them. It was a real life lesson, to never wait again for something that I really wanted, whether it was to meet someone or to say something. I guess that carried into my label situation after that.

I thought I had leverage because of *everything* that I was doing, and I thought I had some power in the deal discussions. In my mind, those boardroom meetings that I was getting shrugs during should have changed by now. I'd broken the sophomore curse, and my third album could be whatever I wanted it to be, along with money to prove they had faith in me. My career was at a high, yet I felt like I was at my absolute lowest with Interscope. You ever get that feeling where everyone is having conversations *about* you, yet it seems like they're never directly asking you what you need? Yeah, that was me. That's how I felt. They were so quick to pop in during my studio sessions to see what I needed to push the album along. Now that it was out in the world and I was moving into the next phase, they didn't really care what I wanted or needed. It felt like I was fighting an uphill battle getting my label to acknowledge the position I was in as we headed into those renegotiations. To be blunt, the bag wasn't what it was supposed to be.

I felt totally disrespected. And not in some neck-snapping, kissing-my-teeth, "you better respect me" kind of way. It was just that I felt like my renegotiations should've been massive. I was bringing them hit after hit. I made that label *a lot* of money. I grew up at Interscope—first signed there as a teenager with Aftermath, then with the Ruff Ryders,

and now I was twenty-three and still there and feeling
super confused about my situation. I was still one of the few
women in hip-hop who were active and at the top of the
charts. I mean, even the men in rap at that time were holding on for dear life to their fame. I was doing something
significant. Paying me what I was worth should've been
a no-brainer, but I just felt...powerless...at a time when
I was theoretically holding all the cards. And beyond the
money, other weird shit had started happening. The label
turned down every creative idea that I was thinking about.
They shot down concepts I had almost immediately. They
also made these odd-ass suggestions. Like in one meeting,
someone turned and said to me, "You know, you should
start wearing more uniforms." *Uniforms.* "That could be
cool," they added. Could it though, really? I didn't think
so. The frustration was building, so I had no choice; I had
to bring out Philly Eve...again. And Philly Eve sought out
the guy with the physical power, the one who talked with
muscle and not manners. If my label wasn't going to pay
me what I was worth, then let me go and show you who I
could bring in to get me my worth! Suge fuckin' Knight!

In retrospect, it was a dumb move, but I had no compass
in this game. I never really had anyone sit me down and
explain the mechanics of the music business, tell me that
women always unfairly get the short end of the stick, even
when they're winning—and that men will always get the
better treatment and be heard a lot faster than women ever
will. I also didn't have anyone empowering *me* specifically.
And maybe I wasn't even empowering myself, instead putting my trust in other people to handle everything. I was
young and I was scared, but I was never really timid, so I
was going to put up *some* kind of fight. The problem was

that I wasn't up on all of the business jargon, so I wasn't able to pull up on my own and start firing off some lingo that they'd all understand (especially when I didn't). I figured that's what I had a lawyer for. I'm a different person now, and I can walk into any meeting and speak with confidence, but I wish back then I'd known just a little more about the business side of things so that I could walk in there and confidently demand action. What was worse, I didn't have anyone really rallying behind me to make things happen. I had a manager (who eventually got his own office in the building—for what? I don't know) and I had me, who had all of these repressed thoughts and feelings that I wanted to shout out loud. But I had more than that too: I also had my talent and my track record.

And now I was about to have the biggest villain in the game with me.

So there I was in Santa Monica that August, cohosting the Soul Train Lady of Soul Awards, when I heard Suge Knight was in the building. I knew what I had to do. I went to my security guard and said, "Hey, can you bring me Suge Knight? I wanna meet him." I don't know who I thought I was, beckoning this man, and my bodyguard thought I was completely insane. He looked at me like, "You can't be serious right now." Oh, but I was. "What's the big deal? Go get him for me!" That was my semidelusional response. The Santa Monica Civic Auditorium was packed for the awards show that night. At one point, I went backstage for a wardrobe change, and when I came back out, the crowd had partially cleared because Suge had showed up. It was crickets when he walked in—complete silence as he entered that building. Everybody knew what time it was. Everybody felt a sense of danger and wanted to run. Everybody but me.

I still didn't see it. I wanted to meet him. My bodyguard chickened out with the intro, so once I saw Suge backstage, I just marched right up to him. "Hi, I've been wanting to meet you," I said to Suge Knight. He was 6'2" with the large build of a retired football player, and even at 5'7" *plus* my heels, I felt like he was a giant. I wasn't scared or nervous though, and he immediately realized it. I knew he was a little shocked by my unwavering confidence. Maybe it was the Philly in me; maybe I was just completely crazy back then.

"Let's go out to dinner," Suge said to me. And so we did. We went to Crustacean in Beverly Hills (Troy came with me), and I've gotta say, Suge was pleasant and really interesting. We had a great time. "What a nice gangster," I thought to myself. The conversation didn't really drift to my label issues until we were nearing our final course at dinner. "So where you at? What's happening?" he asked, alluding to my situation at Interscope. That's when I laid it down for him. I'm up for renegotiations, they're not trying to pay me, I'm not really feelin' it. I had my list of grievances ready for him. "Well, if you need any help, let me know…" he said matter-of-factly. "I'll do whatever." There it was, the offer I was looking for. So I cautiously replied, "…Maybe?"

Now, when I think about it in hindsight, I say to myself, "Um, what the fuck, Eve? Why did you think that would help in any way, shape, or form?" But desperate times call for desperate measures. Plus, when I told my manager, Troy, he didn't flinch at the idea, either. *He* was the one who was more or less sitting in on all those label business meetings about me and heard some of the conversations that I didn't hear. So for him to be okay with my accepting help from the Suge Knight? Well, in my mind, it felt like maybe it was a good idea, after all. And I've gotta say, I was still in my little mood about Dre, even though we made a solid hit together, so having Suge—his former boss at Death Row—stomping around Interscope felt like some sweet revenge. Again, I'm not really sure how I concocted this idea, yet here we were. Maybe Suge felt the same way.

He delivered on his promise and pulled up to Interscope's office in LA one day, as planned. I still don't know what went down the day Suge Knight walked into Jimmy Iovine's office to fight on my behalf. I don't know what kind of threats he was talking or what Jimmy's reaction was. You have to remember in a situation like that, to me it's like gangster versus gangster, since in my mind Jimmy was his own kind of G. It could've played out like a movie scene for all I know. After that, Jimmy went quiet with me. I can't really say I had much dialogue with him. In the few moments that we did, that face-off was never brought up. How would I look if I said, "Oh hey, did Suge stop by?" That would've made about as much sense as my initial plan. Even years later, when I was sitting at Jimmy's house for lunch one day, neither of us ever mentioned that moment. I do know that he wasn't happy after that, and that it definitely didn't help me get my point across. Instead, I feel like he took his anger out on my third album.

Meanwhile, Suge didn't exactly ask me for anything in return, but he started sending a lot of red gifts to my house. Red plants, red furs…he's a Blood, in case you forgot. Maybe my red hair was a green flag for him too. We hung out a few times, but our time together didn't last very long because one day I got a call from Dee and he wasn't pleased. Neither was Waah. They didn't like the idea of me hanging out with Suge at all. The Ruff Ryders guarded me with their lives around your everyday scrawny-ass, nonviolent dudes. But imagine how they felt about me kickin' it with Suge Knight? "All I'm gonna say to you is if he puts his hands on you, we goin' to war," Dee said. "So you need to stop seeing him immediately." I still trusted Dee and Waah with my life, and if Dee said Suge was trouble, then he was trouble. Suge had that whole auditorium scared at his presence and I'd thought nothing of it, but when my guys said it was time to cut the cord, I didn't think twice. I was like, "Okay, cool." I promptly called Suge to break the news to him that we couldn't see each other anymore. We had only hung out a few times, but I had to let him know that we had to stop immediately. He got it, instantly. He said to me, "Listen, if you were my little sis, I would tell you the exact same thing. Respect."

And so we never spoke again.

That was the worst possible way to enter into *Eve-Olution*. My love for the process was fading, and I could just tell that after that Suge situation, the label started distancing themselves. I kind of see why, but come on now, I was still one of their top artists. They should've done what they tell women to do when they're offended: Walk it off. Get back to work. Suck it up. Whatever. It didn't play out that way for me, yet there was still this urgency placed upon me to keep going and make another album. It's not the best headspace to be in when you feel that you're now underpaid, undervalued and ignored—but overperforming. The studio became work for me; it just stopped being fun. And when it's *supposed* to be the place where you find the most joy and now it's not there anymore, it can be a little heartbreaking. Ironically, what I had going for me was that the label didn't seem to care as much anymore, so *now*

I was able to experiment a bit. For that reason, I call *Eve-Olution* my "experimental" album. I still didn't fly off the deep end with ideas, but I started to feel this shift in my consciousness as a songwriter and as an artist. Hip-hop as a whole had changed into *such* a different place than it had been, even within the few years since I entered. So much was happening, *too much*, and not a lot in the way of evolution. I didn't want that for myself traveling deeper into the new millennium, so I made it a point to start really shaking shit up. There's a sense of independence to this album that I didn't have with the one before. There were no A&Rs telling me not to do something. No big label decisions. I still had all of the bells and whistles of being on a major, but with none of the pushback. Who would have thought that an artist's creative freedom could come from the seeming apathy of their record label? I leaned into it, though. And all Suge call-ins aside, I was growing up. I started in my teens and now I was in my twenties. I wanted to bring in more types of music, from some of the other genres that I was into. I wanted to think differently about my samples. I wanted my songwriting to change. What I wanted was more complexity, and I got that.

I asked Prince if I could sample his song "Irresistible Bitch" for my album track "Irresistible Chick," and he told me that I could have the sample for free as long as I didn't curse on my song. *For free.* He had converted and become a Jehovah's Witness by then, so he didn't want the curse words happening, and since I grew up with my grandma who was a Jehovah's Witness, I totally understood. I was not going to fight Prince on that, or anything else for that matter. Ever since we had worked together on his song, he'd been like, "Whatever you need, and whenever you need it, just let me know. I've got you." Crazy to think I had Prince on speed dial yet my label seemed like they were checked out. It was better that way anyway, because I could make even more changes to my whole process.

Scorpion was mainly recorded in Miami, but for *Eve-Olution* I was with the Ruff Ryders out in LA. X was doing another album and the Lox were in and out too, recording. We had rented this big studio that we took over in the Valley, but this time there weren't so many of the other Ruff Ryder crew members around. For me, creatively, I preferred it. I didn't want anyone hanging out in the studio like the old days, and since the label execs weren't hanging around anyway, I could call the shots and have it just be me writing with whatever producer I was working with. That became my comfort zone. But there was also something else changing within the camp, where it wasn't like all of the Ruff Ryders were charging in like gangbusters to come chill. We had all become individual artists, making our individual music in our individual ways. It felt different to me. I still had some of the guys with me on the music. Jadakiss and Styles P were on "Double R What," with Swizz on production, but that was like one of the only true "Ruff Ryders" joints on the album. Swizz produced one other track ("Party In The Rain" with Mashonda), but I had producers like Bink! on there, and the Trackmasters. I added "Satisfaction" with Dre on the beat toward the end and it became a single, and was later nominated for a Grammy for Best Female Rap Solo Performance. But the big hit off *Eve-Olution* was "Gangsta Lovin'" with Alicia Keys. We dropped that at the perfect time during the summer, and Irv Gotti's beat only made it hotter. Plus, I *love* Alicia, and getting to film the music video with her was a lot of fun. I was a Day One fan of Alicia Keys. I went to see one of her earliest shows at Hard Rock Café in Hollywood. I met her after the concert, and I knew at some point that I wanted to collaborate with her. I'm glad we got the chance. That's one of the things that I remain so grateful for: getting to collaborate with artists that I'm an actual fan of. So "Gangsta Lovin'" really added to *Eve-Olution* for a number of reasons.

The album still hit the top ten of the Billboard 200. Critics liked how I'd experimented, and even without the label involved, I hoped they saw that. The happiness I eventually began to feel while making *Eve-Olution* was short-lived, though. Little did I know that it would be the very last album I would release on Interscope and with the Ruff Ryders.

In the moment, though, I was just happy I'd finished it. I was officially ready to take a break, but instead, Hollywood came calling.

11

PLATINUM PLAQUES TO SILVER SCREENS

I'd like to believe that my first real acting role happened in high school, when I hired a crackhead to play the role of my aunt. My mother was pregnant with my little brother, and I took full advantage of that by skipping first period every day (and any other classes that I could) because she was in no condition to come hunt me down. I skipped so much that eventually I wasn't allowed back into school without being signed in by a family member. Enter crackhead. Listen, anytime you need anything—including a stand-in family member—your local neighborhood crackhead is *ready* to provide for you. I asked a guy I used to see around to help me find one of his friends to play my aunt. And he found someone. So I paid this lovely woman five dollars to come to school and just stand next to me as my aunt, while I played the greatest acting role that I had to date.

Now, I had also played some minor roles in the past, like back in elementary school when I wrote a school essay that convinced everyone that my grandfather was cousins with Martin Luther King, Jr., and I won an award for it. But playing the role of MLK's cousin's granddaughter was minor compared to this role of the niece with a troubled aunt. "Miss Jeffers, this person is not a member of your family," the principal said sternly about my "aunt." I returned a shocked expression, while a complete stranger stood next to me, waiting to sign my aunt's name and just be done with this whole ordeal. I found all of the passion I could muster within myself to say, "How *dare you* say that? Just because my aunt is going *through* something doesn't mean she's not a part of *my family*!" I felt that I was totally believable, but my principal was stubborn. They did let me back into school, but I'm still waiting on my award for *that* performance. Being allowed back was not a reward to me.

At least my "aunt" made five dollars.

I had no real interest in acting when the idea was first brought to me as an adult. I didn't imagine myself being in Hollywood, leading that kind of a life. I was a rapper—I wanted to rap. If I did move onto something else, it would be singing, a clothing line, and other stuff. Mainly I just wanted to make music, at least at that point. When I was going into creating *Eve-Olution*, another rapper called me one day to ask me to fill in for a role he was turning down—ironically, in a movie that he was producing. "I got the part and I turned it down," he told me. I mean, *of course* he got the part. It was his own film. But he wanted me for it instead. "I think you'd be really good for it," he told me, to which I was like, "Yeah, but... Nah, I've gotta finish this album." He was one of the first people to see a vision for my acting, but in my mind, I didn't think you could be a rapper *and* an actor. There was definitely this progression, where everybody but me started to see that I had some acting potential. I wasn't on board just yet.

But my manager, Troy—being a Philly native too—came from Will Smith's camp with Overbrook Entertainment. He'd seen firsthand what that pivot looked like and how successful it could be. But he was also playing the long game, knowing that entertainment is a road with many detours and exits. Music is the start, but then there is fashion, there is film, there are perfume lines and whatever else you want beyond the microphone. In his mind, that path was the blueprint for real success when it comes to talent. He saw that with Will Smith, and in working with me, he had a similar goal in mind. He thought the best progression was from hip-hop to pop and then Hollywood. It seemed like a good move when he laid down the facts, and then before I knew it, a random acting role fell in my lap. I was in LA at the right place and the right time when we got the phone call: "Is Eve in LA? And does she want to act?" It was for a role in the movie *xXx* with Vin Diesel, as this character named J.J. I said, "Vin Diesel? I don't know who that is, but sure." Samuel L. Jackson was also in the movie, and I wanted to meet *him*. He ended up getting mad at me on set, because I was so nervous and started improvising my lines. But I couldn't stop cursing, and it was a PG-13 film. It was such a small role, and here I was messing up production trying to improv with profanity. Eventually Samuel himself had to tell me to stop cursing to get through my lines. But hey, it was my very first role! Originally the role was meant for another rapper, but he got sick and it ended up in my hands. So, my first role was an accident. That was the second time that I was the person who came to mind to fill in for a male rapper. It made me feel like I was really blowing past gender barriers, because when they thought of a rapper in general, they thought of me—even if it was to fill in for the last guy.

The thing about it though, was at the time, rappers were just being asked to show up in shit—TV shows, movies, whatever. Rappers had cameos, like, *everywhere*. I naturally just started getting calls from Hollywood, which was perfect timing—I was planning my next moves anyway. After that started happening, though, I told Troy that if I was going to act, then I had to *really* learn how to do it. I saw a lot of rappers who walked onto these sets and thought they could instantly act when they definitely couldn't. I wasn't going to be added to that list. So I signed up for acting lessons. When I met my acting coach, Tracey Moore (who worked with all of the A-list rappers turned actors), the first thing I said to her was, "Okay, so I don't know how to act, and I don't even know if I really want to act." Better to be honest, right? She said to me, "Well, every time you do a music video, you're acting." She shut me right up with that response. Tracey changed my mind and my whole perspective on acting, because yeah, I *was* acting in my music videos. I was playing out the stories of my songs. And the thing was, in my music videos (especially ones like "Love Is Blind"), I did want a story arc and I did want to play a role. Was I a decent actor all along? Maybe? After that conversation, I was like, "Okay, let's go!"

Troy and I picked up and moved to LA (my second time doing so). Before that, I was in New York the whole time and he was back in Philly. But to be honest, even though I moved directly across the country, I was still skeptical. I expected to just keep turning down acting roles and then end up having no opportunities, because I still didn't even know if I wanted to act. There might have been some insecurities around not knowing if I could be great, though a safe space for me would be if I could play a role that was close enough to my actual self. Then the script for *Barbershop* happened. When I auditioned for *Barbershop*, it was the first time I'd read a script and *really* understood it.

The day that I auditioned, I was nervous as all hell. My coach, Tracey, became my friend, and so she came with me to the audition, up until the moment I walked through the door. She understood my anxiety so well, and right before she was like, "Let's get a glass of wine." She didn't have me get drunk or anything—it was just half a glass of white wine, and we got to talk for a bit before I headed inside. She reminded me, "You've got this. You're talented. Let yourself shine through." Tracey's pep talk (and the wine) helped me feel so much better. Once I got inside for the audition, they had me do my lines with a few other cast members, but part of it was all of us just improvising. It felt like the cypher again, and suddenly I was back in my element. I really believe that's how I landed the role.

So I took it. That switch in my understanding of acting was thanks to my coach, but also just seeing the character for who she was and investing in her. I loved playing the role of Terri Jones; I related to her. I *knew* her. She could've been one of my friends. Little did I know that I would even get to grow with her for years. For that initial role, though, they made us take barbershop lessons, so that we could appear more believable. They wanted us to learn how to hold the scissors correctly and use the clippers and stuff. I mean, I wouldn't typically let anyone trust me with a pair of scissors to cut their hair, but I guess I kind of loosely learned how. My homeboy was brave enough to come to the barber school and let me cut his hair for the demonstration. It was just a quick shape-up, though. Outside of that, I still can't cut hair.

In the first scene where you actually meet Terri (and her missing apple juice), I broke the window on a door by accident. I was so embarrassed. It's during the scene where Terri finds out her bottle of apple juice is empty in the refrigerator in the back room of the barbershop, so I had to swing the back door when I stormed back out. I did that a little too well and broke the damn window, but hopefully that helped everyone understand how passionate I was about Terri and her apple juice.

With *Barbershop*, though, something did click for me, and I started taking acting more seriously. I had a trailer and the full movie set experience, which was new and so exciting. I think deep down I knew that my goal was never going to *just* be hip-hop. And it's not because I didn't love it, but because I always kind of had that "what's next?" mentality about me. I didn't want to stay in one place in my work; I just knew that entertainment was where I wanted to be. That didn't necessarily have to just be rapping, though I also didn't want to be pushed into something else that wasn't on my watch. I was getting enough of that with my record label. But *Barbershop* spoke to me. I got to see Ice Cube and his continued evolution into acting right before my eyes, and that inspired me. Plus, who knew the franchise would end up being such a classic? I just wasn't sure I would ever find another role that I could relate to or love.

When the idea of moving over to television came, I told Troy the same thing: if I didn't absolutely love the role and if I didn't relate to the character, then I wasn't gonna do it. The very next script that came was for a sitcom called something like *The Opposite Sex*, and it was on UPN. I was going to have the starring role as a character named Shelly Williams, who was a fashion designer on the dating scene. I loved this character and was down to do it, because I could literally see myself as Shelly. I could play her. She just made sense to me. So before I knew it, I had my own sitcom. Eventually, though, by the time the show was announced, everyone just started calling it "The Eve Show," which led corporate to be like, "Okay, well let's just call it *Eve*," since as the star I was the draw anyway. That didn't make much sense to me. I really wanted to keep the title as it was, but I was only twenty-four and didn't know how to really fight for things like that just yet—even if the new show title confused the viewers. I did ask them if we could change it, and they just fed me this rationale like, "Well, *The Cosby Show* was the Huxtables and Bill Cosby was the star…" Blah blah blah. I kind of just gave up and went with it. The important thing, though, was that since my name was on the show and I was the star, Troy fought for me to be an executive producer as well, which was a game changer for women in hip-hop back then. Queen Latifah had a development deal when she did *Living Single* in the '90s, but since then the opportunities had been limited for girls like us. I was so grateful to Troy for fighting to incorporate that into my deal, because it gave me some power and leverage behind the show. It also allowed me to be part of those deeper conversations in boardroom meetings, where the real decisions were being made.

It was a great opportunity for me…well, when I wasn't screwing it all up.

For the first year and a half of making *Eve*, I completely lost my footing with my career—yet again. I was still very

much acting like a rapper after we wrapped, and then attempting to be a serious actress with her own sitcom after
a night out. It became this vicious cycle. That doesn't work
out at all, to say the least. I was still going to clubs like *every*
night, trying to be this Hollywood rapper-slash-actor, when
really the two can cancel each other out if they're not handled correctly. We would have these table reads at 9:00 a.m.
on Friday mornings. Meanwhile, I'd be out at the club until
four or five in the morning and be rushing to work half-
dead for a table read. It wasn't smart at all, but that transi-
tion for me was so hard. There were good things about it,
and there were bad. I would get up (after what little sleep
I'd had that night) and think to myself, "Damn, I'm getting
in my car and driving to the same place every day." There
was a monotony to it that kind of messed with my head,
before the show even started. Before that, I was always on
the road nonstop, and every day was a different scenery.
The cities changed, the stages, the people. Even going to
the studio to record didn't feel as monotonous as that drive
up to the studio lot to film, like I was heading to my office as an accountant. But there I was, at the equivalent of
my *day job*, which we're technically trying to avoid when
we sign up to be entertainers. At least that was my logic.
It was a mind fuck. The good part about it, though, was
I did have some stability in my life for the first time since
my rap career really took off. I had a home with actual fur-
niture in it. I could walk into my own place again, and it
wasn't just a damn bed and a TV set. There was a sense of
security, even though the process was feeling mundane to
me. I tried fighting the boredom of that routine by being
totally reckless during my off hours. I don't know how I
thought that would ever work, because really everything
turned reckless after that.

LEFT:
At the start of it all, with my mom.
Photo courtesy of the author.

BOTTOM:
Me and my aunt Karen. Wish she could see me now.
Photo courtesy of the author.

TOP:
Me and my cousin Takeya.
Photo courtesy of the author.

BOTTOM RIGHT:
Me and my baby bro Farrod.
Photo courtesy of the author.

I've always been in first place.

All photos courtesy of the author.

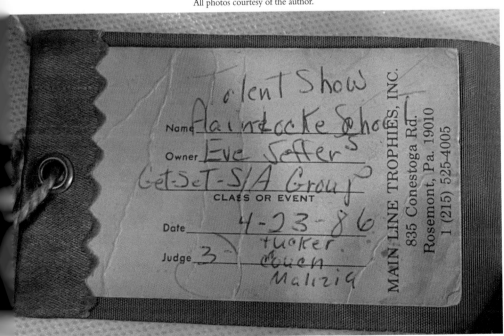

TOP RIGHT:
The fact that I made it to wear that cap and gown… Too bad I didn't get to walk down the aisle and throw it in the air.

Photo courtesy of the author.

BOTTOM RIGHT:
Now *this* is my graduation in my eyes.

Photo credit: Vince Bucci/Getty Images

Young me in the studio, scarf on, ready to write. Let's go.
Photo courtesy of the author.

Me, Kiss and X. Remember them days?
Photo courtesy of the author.

TOP RIGHT:
The yellow-pad lyrics from when I wrote "Let Me Blow Ya Mind." Emphasis on "I wrote it."
Photo courtesy of the author.

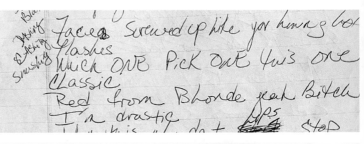

MIDDLE RIGHT:
My Ruff Ryders chain going into the American Museum of Natural History.
Photo courtesy of Kathy Iandoli.

BOTTOM:
Me and my girls on *The Talk*. Missing Julie here.
Photo courtesy of the author.

Battle ready.

It wasn't *all* my fault, though. In my defense, there was a lot of pressure working on my own sitcom. I was the youngest person on set, and I was the star. Everyone else was either getting married or like having their first baby, buying their first houses. They were just so settled down, while the only constant for me was the sitcom and then showing up to the same club each night with real consistency. I wasn't at the same point in life as everyone else on set, and I was definitely not as settled down as they all were. It made my moves look even *worse* by comparison, because they were looking like responsible adults, and I was looking like a person who didn't know what the hell she was doing. I would throw these big after-parties in my dressing room, which did me no favors the next morning. Really, though, it was just all so unnecessary. It really felt like I was leading a double life. By day I was this sitcom actress, and by night I was a rapper, ballin' in the clubs and drunk as hell.

My first year, I really felt like a fish out of water when it came to production. Maybe it was a little bit of impostor syndrome, but it was overwhelming. Naturally, the partying didn't help, but so much of it was me learning how to acclimate in an entirely new world. I was shocked to learn that some sitcoms have "professional laughers," people who come in a few times a week to "laugh" so that the laugh tracks can be recorded, but also to see which jokes would land. It was bizarre. Coming from hip-hop, where "keep it real" was drilled into my brain, seeing how on TV even laughter was manufactured at times was a wakeup call. Even though the laughter was fake at times, the cast and crew and I were very real. I remember my makeup artist on the show, Rea Ann Silva, applied my makeup by cutting up small sponges into different pieces to apply my makeup. "Don't tell anyone, but I'm working on my own set of sponges," she told me one day. Rea Ann later invented the Beauty Blender. We were all a part of each other's lives in different ways.

Filming *Eve* was such a "family" environment, which was another new experience. You're spending so much time with people consistently on set that you do become a little family. Natalie Desselle-Reid (may she rest in peace) used to make us this amazing monkey bread. We'd spend birthdays together (I used to hire magicians to come perform), Super Bowl parties, housewarmings, new babies, everything. This was the cast *and* the crew. We would even have Karaoke Thursdays, which were so much fun!

I was shocked it lasted three seasons, what with the way everything was going on. I eventually felt a little more balanced with it toward the end, but by then it was just too late. I don't really believe in having regrets, but I will say if there is one thing in my life that I do regret, it's not taking *Eve* as seriously as I should have. It was an amazing experience with an incredible ensemble cast. The show was nominated for awards, and so was I for my acting. There was real potential there, but the timing wasn't right. I wish I had put my own foot down (or in my ass) and taught myself some discipline. I blame myself for the show not getting a fourth season. I really feel like my behavior contributed to that, because whether it was those after-parties in the dressing room or barely making it to table reads, I was screwing up. Sometimes *because* of those damn parties, I would miss a read-through the next day. All bad.

I stacked my plate too high. I was also filming both *Barbershop* and, later, *Barbershop 2* around that time, and also started putting together my Fetish clothing line. And while the *Barbershop* franchise was definitely helping to shape me as an actor, that was just way too much to have going on simultaneously. I went from not really knowing if I even wanted to be an actor to having my own sitcom and filming two movies. Well, three with *xXx*. That's how it tends to happen with my life, though. It's like a flood or a drought, so naturally the moment I say "maybe" to acting, every role comes flying at me, and before I knew it, my professional life was turned upside down. There was just so much going on personally too.

As a human, I was having another shift. I couldn't keep up with who I was, but I just kept trying and trying. I was like six or seven years deep into a career that became the only life that I knew how to live. I tried to combat that by fusing my two worlds together, when in reality those were two very different lifestyles. Also, I didn't know how to just be home, going to work the next day. The residual life in the fast lane was still speeding through me. Ironically, being so stable, with a home to come back to, led me to go out and drink even more. On the road, I'd been partying *less*, since I never wanted to be drunk onstage or when I was making my music. So having that home base actually led to even worse behavior, as strange as that may sound. It's crazy to think that having a place to be grounded left me anything *but* that—and that's when the warning signs around my drinking first started showing. I learned a valuable lesson, though. When you choose to act, then you have to make that switch. You have to learn how to discipline yourself and lead a whole new life while you're filming. I have so much respect for my fellow actors, because I know what it took for me to become one. Again, that was a pretty turbulent time all around, because I was dealing with a lot.

And I do mean *a lot*...

12

STRANGE FETISHES

This was not how I wanted to see myself on the internet. Even worse, the day that thirty-second clip of me leaked online, it was like every news outlet was talking about it. I briefly became a headline. A DJ from one of the big radio stations was the first to call me and tell me about it, and that's when I went online and saw what was happening. The stories referenced my past relationship, which I didn't ever want to think about again. They even talked about my two months dancing, like this was all some career path for me. I was horrified, I was embarrassed, and I was hurt. I was in another relationship by then, yet there I was with my ex, on full display. It was one of the most violating feelings that I have ever experienced, and it made me sick to my stomach. I already had my suspicions about who'd leaked it, but I didn't want revenge.

I wanted answers.

I hired a private investigator, one who I knew had some connections in the adult film industry. He had access to some of the people who ran the major websites, especially ones where celebrity sex tapes were uploaded. Sometimes the celebrities "leaked" the tapes themselves; other times they were passed off and leaked by another person (usually someone they knew...sadly). I most definitely didn't leak a clip of myself, but with one of the websites the investigator was able to check with the site owner to find the name of the person who'd passed the original clip off and had it uploaded. When he called me with the name of the person, it was exactly who I'd thought it was. The person's full government name was listed right there as the owner, and I will leave it at that. I was so disgusted. It was filmed seven years prior, right around the time that I had my nervous breakdown. Even though it was less than a minute long, it brought me back to a terrible time in my life. It was triggering to say the least. The thing nobody tells you about these situations is that once it's out there, *it's out there*. Thankfully, this wasn't in the era of social media, so it didn't become as widespread as it might have just a few years later. It gets harder and harder to contain something on adult sites once it's out there, though, so by the time I really launched an investigation, the clip had already been passed off to someone else, who kept it moving like wildfire. Meanwhile, I was starring on a television series, I was starring in movies—now I was starring in *this*. It had to be stopped.

Within a week of the clip leaking, I got a call out of the blue from an infamous mob wife; somehow this clip had landed in her lap. She said to me, "I can make this disappear for you." I was a little scared, but a little intrigued too. She asked me to come see her in New York City. This wasn't an ultimatum or anything, but I knew I couldn't just be like, "Nah, no thanks." So I agreed to it. When I called my friend in the industry and told him, he was like, "Oh hell no, you're not going there alone. I'm pullin' up too!" I've always been lucky to have good guys like that around me (more than the few snakes) who always want to protect me. So then we both headed to this restaurant in the city to see her. About a week after that, I got a call from the mob wife again. She said to me, "You know, in my experience, it's just better to pay these people. If you pay them, it'll probably just go away." I said to her, "Really? Why should I pay them? I don't think I should be paying them *any* money!" She said, "Yeah, well, you're a public figure, so you probably should just pay them and get it over with."

When I told the man I was involved with at the time, he said the same thing. "Yeah, just pay them. It'll go away." Part of me felt like since he was high-profile, he just didn't want that news to travel, but whatever—I didn't think I owed anyone anything. I told Troy the whole story, and he said, "Man, fuck that shit! We don't have to pay anybody!" So weeks later, we got the cops involved, who brought the FBI into the investigation. They arranged this "payoff" to the man holding the footage and made sure it crossed state lines (from New York to New Jersey) to make it a federal case. After the pickup of the so-called payment was arranged, the man was arrested. And that was the end of that.

Sometimes the clip is mentioned, and I just kind of roll my eyes, but one reference to it in particular felt especially unnecessary. It was years after the clip had leaked, and I was a guest on *Fashion Police* on E! Apparently, another celebrity sex tape had just leaked, and the late Joan Rivers turned to me like, "What's wrong with you kids and your sex tapes?" I was furious. First of all, don't lump me in with a group of celebrities who film sex tapes for the public to watch (and I told her that). Second, it was *years* ago, and it had been leaked against my will (I told her that too). It wasn't hard to see that I was offended; to corner me about it had definitely not been the move, not when I had put it so far behind me. I never wanted that moment to repeat itself, especially not on national television when I was supposed to be talking about fashion. Kelly Osbourne actually came up to me after we filmed to apologize.

And it wasn't just that the clip had leaked—it was the timing of when it happened. I was acting in all of these projects, and I was just getting my clothing line off the ground. Why *then*? But isn't that always when the devil strikes the hardest? Like always, though, I just kept going. It didn't affect my career, thankfully, especially since the whole situation was so gross and violating to begin with. So instead of dwelling on it, I just kept the machine running and kept working through my goals.

Fetish, my clothing line, was something that definitely made sense to launch in the middle of my acting career, especially with the role I was playing on TV. My character Shelly was a fashion designer on *Eve*, and I really had always wanted to have a clothing line. Troy first brought it to the table as another part of my longevity plan, and I loved it. But like with everything else, I needed to *fully* know what I was getting into. I had to know *everything* about the process, and I had to speak with people who already did it and had had success doing it. I knew I had to go all-in or else it wouldn't work.

So what did I do first? I called Puffy.

I said, "Hey, can I take you out to lunch?" He was like, "Why?" I replied, "I have some questions to ask you." I met him at Cipriani's, and when we got there I broke out my notebook and my pen and said to him, "I'm starting my own clothing line, and I have some questions about how you started Sean John." He was in shock. He said, "You really are here, taking me out to lunch, to ask me questions about how I started my clothing line?" Philly Eve jumped out to reply, "Yeah! What the fuck else did you think I wanted?" He was like, "Nah, I'm just saying! That's so funny. I respect it." I guess no one ever pulled up on Puffy to feed him and ask him business questions, but that's just my personality. I even called Jay-Z and had a bunch of questions ready about Rocawear. He was equally in shock. I think it was Puff who gave me the piece of advice that if I was going to launch my line, I had to be as involved as possible in the process.

I launched Fetish during the first season of *Eve*, and it really took off, because there weren't any other women in hip-hop with their own clothing lines. Jennifer Lopez started her J.Lo line a few years before, and like two years after Fetish, Kimora Lee launched Baby Phat, but I am proud to have been a pioneer in that space. It did cost me a lot of money, though. Too much. I can definitely say now that I spent more than I made, but seeing my line in department stores like Macy's, having billboards all over New York City, and getting to be a part of the fashion world with my own brand was definitely cool. I worked with the art director, who also did the J.Lo line. Our ad layouts were high-level and we worked with some of the best photographers for our shoots. That was how I wanted it. It had to look sharp and high fashion. But all that is expensive, so yeah, my money was being poured into the operation in the name of quality. I had some business partners, though, and I'm pretty sure they made money off it. To be honest, I think I just didn't ask the right questions throughout the process—didn't know enough about it all. Ironically, I could sit at lunch with my peers and ask every question in the book about conceptualizing a clothing line, but once it came down to the business parts, I left that to my manager. I was in love with the creative aspect of it all. I took part in every meeting about that, even down to the stitching on a pair of jeans. But when it came to the business part of really looking after what was going out and what was coming in, I just didn't have the words. I didn't have the vocabulary. I didn't have the courage to speak up. And I really believed that everyone else involved had my back. I believed for such a long time that in this industry, the people you hire (which ends up being mostly *men*) must know better than you and must always have your best interests in mind. That's how it's supposed to be, but that sadly isn't always the case. I stopped trusting the process and the people involved. Production timelines weren't being met (which slows *everything* down), and it led to product not being delivered. After about a year, I felt it collapsing, and so I found a new partner with Marc Ecko's company Eckō Unlimited.

I needed to feel like I had someone there with my best interests in mind, so I asked my mom to come work for me in New York at my office. She had prior fashion experience and knew the lay of the land—she was even a model when she was younger—so I hired her as my proxy. She would basically be me while I was gone, whether I was filming or touring or anything else, and she was the liaison for the design team. She was also my spy. I needed all eyes on that operation, because something just wasn't adding up. I told her, "Mom, I need you to watch whatever's going on over there. Keep an eye on them." And she did. The people there loved having my mom in the office, and she really loved being there too. But I guess not *everyone* wanted her eyes on what was going on, because they did something so terrible that I still can't believe how it all went down: one of the partners fired her without my knowing it. She was so upset, especially with the way it all happened. Basically, he was so disgusting and disrespectful to her, and he hurt her feelings. To this day, I swear that man better not find himself in a room with me again after how he acted with my mother. I had to find out from my mom that she was fired a few days later, when she'd thought I'd known all along. When I called her one day to ask about business, she said, "Wait, you don't know?" I said, "Know what?" And that's when she told me. My partners didn't even have the respect to call me and say, "Hey, your mother isn't suited for this position." After that, things started slowly unraveling. It was a waiting game, where I was at the mercy of the company. My line was ultimately shelved, right as so much else was going on in my personal and professional life. There was a part of me that wanted to be done with it, but then another part of me that didn't. In the worlds of hip-hop and fashion, it was a boys club. And then there was me. I didn't want to give up on the company. It was doing well and people loved it. Signature Apparel reached out to partner with me, so in my mind there was a second chance and I went with it. By then, I felt a little more empowered. I knew a little more about the business, and I started making some demands that I probably should have made from the beginning. I asked for better-quality fabrics, new designs, everything.

I did that for about two more years, but I started to feel like the company wasn't focused on it. They had other lines that were getting all of their attention; meanwhile, mine was seemingly left out. They weren't building any hype around it, and once you go from being really out there to being shelved, the next go-round has to bring an even bigger awareness. That just wasn't happening. I was losing steam with it—the whole process. It wasn't long before I had to move on for good. I walked away from Fetish, and in hindsight that wasn't a good decision. I should have kept it going, but after everything I had been through with it, I wasn't thinking clearly.

To this day, when I see some pieces that I have left from the Fetish line or people tell me they still have their Fetish jeans—the ones I made sure looked perfect in every meeting I sat in—I'm proud. I think about all of our old billboards and the pieces that people have kept, and it makes me happy that I did it and made history. I accomplished something major with my line (and for the first time), and kept it running for a long time—even while I was struggling with my acting schedule and even through my name wrongfully showing up in the tabloids. If I could do it all again (which I hope to), I think I would ask more questions and be more aggressive with my decisions. I would be careful about whom I trusted, and I would put more faith in my own gut feelings rather than just assuming that everyone else knew more than I did. It was my company, after all, but sometimes your empowered moments can be viewed as "cute" rather than intimidating by the men around you.

Sometimes they don't even look at you during those meetings; they look through you. And while I was business savvy, I just didn't have that cutthroat mentality about me. I knew how to work hard, learn about everything, and get the job done. But sometimes men have a real *fetish* for undermining women. Back then, sadly, I let them do it. Lesson learned, though, because sometimes you have to go through something to really understand it and grow from it. I was a different person back then and didn't have the confidence to ask the questions that warranted answers. I underestimated my own insight and intuition, and so I got taken advantage of in so many different ways. Those days are long gone, though. Try doing that to me now.

I dare you.

13

THINGS FALL APART

It had been years since we were all in a room together, let alone standing side by side onstage as a whole Ruff Ryders family. And yet there we all were at the Barclays Center in Brooklyn on April 25, 2021, reunited at last. But one of us was missing…at least in the physical sense.

After his death on April 9 of that year, I found it so hard to believe that DMX was really gone. I'd check in on X through Swizz over the years, asking for updates on how he was doing and what he was up to. In the months leading up to his passing, it seemed as though he was doing much better. He was happier and healthier, Swizz told me. That made me so happy to hear. He stayed in my prayers no matter what, because no matter where we were in life, that was my family. We were all supposed to come together again that fall for a Ruff Ryders reunion tour, especially since X had been getting better, but that would never happen. Now we were saying goodbye to him forever. DMX fought so many demons within himself for so long, and even while he fought them, he still managed to win the world over. He had a charm to him that other rappers struggled to replicate. There was a warmth about him that brought people to tears when he hit the stage. He made magic. To me, he was on the cusp of something massive when he was at the height of his career. He had hip-hop sitting in the palm of his hands, and he was in Hollywood doing the movie thing. He was well on his way to rock star status. That alone can put too much pressure on someone, but add in all that he was going through internally and the road wasn't easy for him. I remember when he came to visit me one time in LA after not seeing each other for a while, and I saw so much pain in his eyes. The demons were winning. But no matter what, I always saw his heart. He was my brother through and through. My only wish for him was that he would have more time—for himself, to enjoy some of the success that he had built over the years, but most importantly, time with his children. X deserved that happiness; Lord knows he earned it. But sometimes that doesn't happen for people while they're on this earth. And as I stood there at his funeral, I couldn't help but feel some relief that his pain was gone and that he was at peace. Addiction is a disease, it *is* the demon, and X was fighting it for a long time. But he didn't have to fight anymore.

Something else happened, though, when we lost DMX: it felt like the spirit of the Ruff Ryders was laid to rest. From that moment on, it would never be the same; the heart of our unit had left us. Losing X felt like the definitive end of an era—the closing of a major chapter in my life, even though that end had been years in the making.

We never had a fight or a falling-out. Nothing like that.

It's not like we all didn't speak either; we just weren't really in each other's lives like we were before. At the beginning of my career, my days and nights were filled with Ruff Ryders—in the houses that we rented, in the studios where we recorded, in the cars we drove, in the clubs we went to. My whole life for years included having some Ruff Ryder around me 24/7, whether it was a road manager, an artist, whomever. The whole routine of having the Ruff Ryders always in my orbit just kind of started tapering off. It was bound to happen eventually in some way, though. We weren't in boot camp anymore as a whole crew. There was no more training for the big event; we *were* the big event. We accomplished that mission that we all set out to when we first came together. I guess you could say we came, we saw, we conquered. We learned and we grew, and then it was time to leave the nest. It was gradual, though. The distance didn't appear overnight. I first started to notice it while I recorded *Eve-Olution* in Los Angeles back in 2002—how I wanted to be alone in my process, without everyone hanging out in the studio with me. It was no longer just tons and tons of guys around for fun. A detachment was forming, at least on my end. I welcomed it, though. I was doing what I was supposed to be doing with my music, and I felt like I didn't need a cosign from the guys anymore. I was my own person; I was my own artist. I was still releasing my music under the Ruff Ryders umbrella, but eventually I was seen as just Eve, and not Eve: the First Lady of the Ruff Ryders. Things started happening for me on a solo level—big things. I was getting booked for daytime TV shows, prime time and late-night, that high-level stuff. I knew Dee and Waah were proud of me, though. I never had any doubt in my mind about that. But even in the midst of all that going on in my solo career, all of the good things, I felt a little lonely without everyone else. It was an adjustment for sure.

From a business standpoint, I always kept my affairs separate. I had entered into the fold with the Ruff Ryders like that. I had my own separate situation with my own manager. Things just felt better to me that way. It was no disrespect to Dee and Waah, but I didn't want my label and my management to be one and the same, with both hands in either of my pockets. That's how I always thought about it. As a signed artist, I also felt like I needed an outside person who could represent me if something popped up, God forbid. In my mind, it was like, "Who would have *my* back?" The guys never fought me on that. It did set me apart from the pack, though, since I was always on a different path from the start. Once I started working with Troy, he and I put our own longevity plan in place for me, where I was moving into TV, movies, fashion…all of those things that happen when you level up. But I did come to a fork in the road, where it seemed like on the business side, the Ruff Ryders checked out and Interscope was tagged in. There was no conversation that was had—or if there was, then I wasn't a part of it. Maybe Troy and Dee or Waah spoke with the label, but I have no idea. The way it felt though, was that they all kind of left me and weren't coming back for me, which added to that lonely feeling. It could have just been a series of business decisions, but on a personal level, I saw it as being left behind. I did expect them to come back to figure this all out and do something to repair my situation, but if we all kind of felt like I was less and less a part of the Ruff Ryders "label" then maybe they just didn't consider me signed to them any longer, even if I was still connected as a crew member.

That period of record label limbo really lacked clarity for me, and as I think about it now, I realize I should have been more aware of what was going on behind closed doors. I was intimidated, though, by anything involving my business affairs. I'd be the first one to speak up about a beat or anything else creative. Those were the things I'd put my foot down and be adamant about, but on the business side of my label dealings (much like my situation with Fetish), I just put all of my trust into other people. I really felt like Troy could handle it on my behalf, until one day he was no longer there, either. We parted ways before the taping of the final season of *Eve* in 2006. Interscope ended up giving Troy his own office, so he was on his own path with them, and in the blink of an eye, I was all alone.

I didn't have the Ruff Ryders; I didn't have Troy. I had me, all by myself, attempting to deal with my record label. I felt like I'd been abandoned at a time when I could have used some people in my corner. That was when the real nonsense began. Interscope started challenging everything I wanted to do for my fourth album. I had *so* many ideas, and I recorded *so* many songs. I had one track where I rapped over the White Stripes' "Seven Nation Army" that would have really been a total contrast to what was going on in rap at the time. They said no to that. I had Mark Ronson wanting to executive produce my whole album. They didn't want that, either. Pharrell wanted to do the same, and it was still a no. I had a song with Will.i.am, one with Mary J. Blige. Nothing.

The label didn't even want "Tambourine"! When I first brought them that song, they listened to it and said, "This is never going to happen." They thought it was *too* pop—*too* Top 40. They didn't believe that "urban" radio would ever latch on to it, even with Swizz on the beat. And yes, "Tambourine" was a "slow burn" record, as they say in the music industry, but urban radio did take it—and they ran with it. That song did its thing all on its own. It grew its own legs, without the label machine marketing it, because my label was clearly backing away from supporting me. They *did* fund the music video, though, which cost $725,000 and was my favorite part of the whole "Tambourine" rollout. I loved doing that video; it was my first time really getting to be creative and I worked a lot with the director Melina Matsoukas. I was obsessed with the Sofia Coppola film *Marie Antoinette* and wanted my own spin on it for "Tambourine." Melina was amazing and helped me bring that vision to life. I mean, she went on to direct the show *Insecure* and do music videos like Beyoncé's "Formation," and her directorial eye has always been sharp. In *Marie Antoinette*, the colors are more muted, with saturated pale colors, so I wanted the video to be bubblegum pink and bright, where you want to just reach your hand right through the screen and touch it. I was lucky the label paid for it, but that was really the end of their investment in me.

By the time I released my song "Give It to You" with Sean Paul, the label had completely stopped working my records altogether. I had no team left at Interscope working on anything pertaining to me. I recorded all of these songs and it felt like the label refused to work any of them. Eventually, the label came to me and said, "You're just going to have to redo all of it." I said to them, "What the hell do you mean? You want me to go back in and record *more* songs? I just recorded *all* of this shit for you!" They simply said, "Yeah, well, we're not feeling any of it." They started putting me in the studio with all of these different people, from producers to artists, recording all of these tracks, and once they came back to them the response was always "No." It became a waste of my time, and my frustration was building. I was doing *everything* they'd asked of me. I went into the studio with the producers they wanted; I worked with the artists they suggested. None of it was good enough. It felt like they stopped believing in me and didn't know where I fit. They had just pushed out Fergie's album after she went solo from the Black Eyed Peas, and had just signed Lady Gaga (who Troy later managed). I felt like the label literally had no clue what to do now with this rap chick—so they opted to just do nothing at all. For me, it's one thing to tie my hands on the business side—things that I had never really known about to begin with—but once you start stifling my creativity, that's when I go into fight mode, and that's what they were doing. It became a nonstop cycle of shooting down my music and making me feel worse and worse.

I felt blackballed. But most of all, I felt so alone—with no manager to pull up to my meetings and speak up for me and no Ruff Ryders to mobilize. As far as I was concerned, there was only one thing left for me to do: I needed to get off Interscope. It doesn't work like that at record labels, an artist can't just up and leave when they're not feeling supported, but I found an easy way out.

Well, sort of.

One of my homeboys who had nothing to do with Interscope called me one day. Apparently, a friend of his had heard that a meeting was being held at Jimmy Iovine's house. I don't really know who all was there, but the goal of the meeting was to figure out who was staying with Interscope and who would be dropped. During that meeting, a list of twenty-five names were brought to the chopping block. Mine was one of them. When my friend told me this news, I was stunned, but I felt like, "Okay, this is what I need." He told me not to say anything, and I turned to him like, "Are you crazy? I have something to hold over Jimmy Iovine's head to get me out of there." I *had* to use it. So I sent Jimmy an email and basically told him that I knew about this meeting. I knew there were twenty-five names on a list, and I knew that mine was one of them. I didn't want to be a part of anyone's big decision about who to keep and who to drop; I wanted to make that decision for myself before they could do it for me. I closed the email with this message: "You should just let me go." Was a part of me calling his bluff? Maybe. But regardless, I couldn't keep going in the direction I was headed in with Interscope. After sending that email, I was ultimately released from Interscope Records. At first it felt good. It felt like I had accomplished what I'd set out to do. If they weren't going to work with me, then they were working against me, so they had to get out of my way. But that triumphant feeling faded very quickly.

Ultimately, leaving Interscope didn't feel as victorious as I had hoped it would. It felt shitty. I spent ten years on that label. I grew up with them. Even through my Aftermath situation and then later with the Ruff Ryders, Interscope was actually the constant throughout. And now they were gone, and I had no record deal. I felt a lot of things, but at the top of the list was feeling like they didn't want me anymore. That hurt the most, like, "Damn, really? This is how my career with Interscope had to end? With a meeting, and a list, and then ultimately just an email? And that's it?" I felt so horrible. It's a terrifying feeling, being signed to a label for your entire career, and then you're just out there as a free agent. It soured me on the whole music industry. It felt like all bullshit—all politics. I kind of had to pause and say, "No thanks." I felt burned-out and betrayed by an industry that I had given so much of myself to.

In the end, my fourth album was shelved by Interscope indefinitely. The "hip-hop lawyer" that I was using at the time didn't seem to handle my renegotiated contract correctly, either. In the contract, the wording suggested that *Eve-Olution* almost didn't exist (or that it was a part of *Scorpion*), so I owed another album on a deal that I'd essentially been dropped from. It really boiled down to the one thing record labels care about, which is publishing rights. My contract fused the publishing rights for two of my albums together, which made no sense whatsoever. This fight lasted well over fifteen years. I had no idea what I was in for when I first sent that email asking to be released from my contract. During that time of turmoil, I recorded a song called "Miss Glass." It's just me, singing. No rapping. In the song I talk about feeling fragile and broken, like I was made of glass. That's really the only way that I can describe how I felt during that time. It's a feeling that I never want to revisit again.

I was lucky, though, because there was a whole other world that was calling my name. I still had Hollywood. And even though there had been that monotony of going to set every day, I started to appreciate that routine, especially with films. I was able to put all the bullshit of the music industry on the back burner and just show up for my filming and get my check. There was a comfort in that. But good ol' Tinsel Town had its own set of problems…

…and I became one of them.

14

HOLLYWEIRD

As I sat in the middle of a group of people at the Church of Scientology, there was only one thought in my mind: "I am *not* eating their lunch!"

No, literally. I don't mean that in the metaphorical "I'm not buying what they're selling" kind of way; I actually thought that their food was somehow laced with something and that I would be knocked out and dragged upstairs to be brainwashed. A little dramatic, yes, but what did I know? I was still new to Hollywood and everything that came with it. I still can't even comprehend how the hell I got to the Church of fucking Scientology in the first place. I was invited to go by a female rap legend, who thought it would be a nice way to introduce me to everyone and get to know the Church. She, apparently, was a Scientologist, and so were her famous friends. And because I love to think that I'm some sort of undercover spy or investigative journalist on assignment, I agreed to go. My curiosity was so high. I mean, I had heard enough about Scientology— rumors about some *interesting* parts, at least—but I felt like I had to go and analyze this Church myself since I was being given this unique opportunity for access. But after arriving, I very quickly wanted to go home.

First of all, the large bright blue building had "SCIEN-TOLOGY" written on the front in big block letters, so I already couldn't take it seriously. It looked like a religious amusement park, but also an asylum. I was going to the "Mother Church," which was the international hub for all of the other Scientology churches. When I got there, they had me park in the leader's parking space. Now I felt like a VIP: a VIP in the Church of Scientology. I was meeting my fellow female rapper friend, along with another friend of hers that worked in television. The Church was holding some event that was doubling as an informational session (at least for me it was). Outside of the guests, everyone else was wearing a uniform, and they were all just walking around like a little friendly army. I very quickly started to realize that I wasn't just being invited for some friendly conversation—I was being recruited. I immediately wanted to run back outside. There were other celebrities in the building, which was crazy to see. A lot of dedicated members. Before I eventually bolted out the door, Kirstie Alley walked in with her two kids. It was a family affair.

When the food arrived, I was too scared to eat it. I didn't think they were going to poison me or something, but they might've sprinkled a little somethin' somethin' in there, where I'd pass out and wake up an expert in Dianetics. I didn't want to be rude, but I also wasn't just going to eat out of courtesy. Not even the ghost of L. Ron Hubbard was going to get me to try their food, but I needed a way out of it—so in a state of panic, I told them that I ate before I came. Sitting through their conversations made me realize that Scientologists take this shit *very* seriously. I sat there completely confused. I'm no stranger to organized religion, but I found myself confused by how I'd ever thought that attending this event would be a good idea. I had to check myself for a moment and ask, "What the hell are you doing? What is your life right now?" I answered that question in my head with a call to action, and promptly got up to head out the door. They fixed me a plate to take home, and as I walked out of the Church of Scientology for the first and last time, I threw the plate into the garbage and ran to my parked car in the leader's space.

Hollywood is different; that's for sure.

Los Angeles in general is not for the faint of heart, especially if you're in the process of sorting things out in your life. You hear these stories of young people traveling to California to "find themselves" and then waiting tables to get into acting. Some make it, and some don't. But I wasn't there to find myself; I was just completely lost. It was an odd twist of fate that I headed to Hollywood while fighting with my record label, with a SAG card in my hand. I didn't know which end was up. That "rapper-slash-actor" title was leaning more in the direction of "actor-slash-rapper," and I wasn't completely comfortable with that shift, even though the stability and money that came from acting were nice. Since my label wasn't cooperating with me or supporting anything that I was doing, the whole routine of living life as a "signed rapper" was fading. It was replaced by auditions, call sheets, and set times—where every new opportunity meant that when the cameras turned on, I had to play an entirely different person. That part was exciting to me, because I didn't know who *I* was anyway, so changing into characters was a lot of fun. I also sensed that I was headed toward a huge life shift. As a result, I left Interscope after almost a decade of being signed. At the same time, I was being swallowed up by the Hollywood lifestyle.

I used to hang out almost every night at this club called Teddy's. It was a small nightclub in the front of the Hollywood Roosevelt Hotel. It had just opened when I first landed in Hollywood, and it was like that cool spot where everyone wanted to be—especially me. Teddy's was hot! At one point, Prince did a whole month of 2:00 a.m. shows there, and I was at every single one of them. I basically lived at Teddy's. I was there so much that I joked with my friends about how I should name my firstborn Teddy. It was that serious. I had some amazing times there. I might look back at it now and call myself a degenerate, but in the moment, it was a vibe. Now, mind you, I was not some washed-up celebrity, just casually trying to hang out somewhere cool. I was entering this equation as the "it" girl—the one who was out there dominating in both hip-hop *and* Hollywood. My songs were on the radio, I was in movies, and I was acting in a bunch of TV shit. I was still pretty much everywhere... especially Teddy's.

Eventually, I just stopped treating Teddy's like it was a "night out," which meant I didn't even get dressed in "club clothes" to go there. While everyone else was all dolled up like this was going to be the most important party night of their lives, I was practically in my pajamas. I felt so comfortable there that I would show up in a Juicy Couture sweat suit with Uggs on my feet. Why did I have to look nice at *Teddy's?* The owners knew me there, and it was like my extended living room. I was above the dress code. It didn't click in my mind that there was something very wrong with finding that much comfort in a nightclub. The truth of the matter was that I hung out at Teddy's because I didn't want to go home.

If I went home then I'd be alone and left to think about things, which I didn't want to do. I didn't want to have my mind going at all, actually. I wanted to be in a state of blankness, where I didn't have to process the fact that things in my life were changing—that *I* was changing. So to combat those feelings, I numbed myself with drugs and alcohol.

This wasn't my first trip down that road. Back in '99— when I was on tour and overwhelmed with my new life, my toxic relationship, and my codependent friendships—I started messing with drugs like ecstasy to get out of my own head. I paired that with weed and liquor, and the combination wreaked havoc on my body and, in addition to everything else going on, caused me to have my nervous breakdown. All of that experimenting and combining different substances just had a field day on my emotions. It led to a chemical imbalance—which led to a really, really horrible spiral.

Eight years later, a similar situation started happening. Life changes were beginning again, and familiar people in my life were leaving. The same emotions and worries were coming back around, and I handled them in almost the exact same way. I was drinking every night, smoking weed, taking Xanax, dabbling with ecstasy again—all just to not think about anything. I was hungover all the time, and even though hangovers suck, at least you can't think straight while you have one. So if I wasn't thinking when I'm drunk or high, and I wasn't thinking when I'm hungover, then I would never be thinking at all. That's how numb I wanted to be. I wanted to be oblivious to the world around me. I didn't want to feel or give a fuck, or care about what was happening. So I became kind of a high-functioning zombie.

Back then, I didn't know what anxiety was. I didn't understand it. There weren't conversations around it like there are now. There were no memes or TikTok videos to teach you about the signs and symptoms, and there was no real community of people telling you that they suffer from it too. And mental health wasn't something that was ever preached to celebrities, as if sanity was the only luxury that we couldn't have. But I can use that word now and say that I suffered from severe anxiety, which is its own gateway drug to depression. I am also sensitive to energies around me, and I was taking in a lot of toxic energy that started turning me toxic too, like it had in my past. I was back to just feeling really, really sad. Hollywood is a *terrible* place to be under anxiety's wicked spell, and when you're working in Hollywood, it's even worse. You still have to function in the eye of the storm, and you can't really look like you're in distress because the cameras will catch you slippin' at some point. It could be on set, in front of the media, or at the mercy of the paparazzi. So I was hiding in plain sight while my emotions were consuming me. I was partying a lot with one friend in particular, who I now know was suffering way more than I was. But we were codependent friends—drinking, drugging, and just trying to dilute the constant anxiety and the sadness that came with it. The thing about any synthetic "cure" is that it's temporary relief for the shit you're going through. The alcohol eventually wears off and so do all the drugs. I didn't sleep a lot during that time, but when I did, I I'd wake up and feel like I'd been punched in the fucking face by my anxiety yet again. The only way to fight it was to reload with more alcohol, more drugs. I was trapped in a cycle, and I didn't know how to handle that. I was just a few years away from turning thirty, and I was already coming to the end of my rope. My solution was to try to escape the prison of my own mind, though that ended up landing me in jail.

"Tambourine" was released not even two weeks before, on April 17, 2007, and we shot the video to accompany the release. My label was in apathy mode, so I knew that our time together was ending, and I was bracing myself for possibly the worst professional breakup of my life. I was still on a constant bender, but on top of that, I'd been taking diet pills to lose weight so that I could look skinny in the "Tambourine" music video. Now I'm hopped up on diet pills, liquor, and whatever else was available. And then my song dropped. Where did I celebrate? Teddy's. On that one fateful night, I announced to everyone there that they were invited back to my house for an after-party. I was living in West Hollywood, close enough to the club that I could just make this open invite for everyone to come over. Not smart. Sean Penn was even there at Teddy's that night and said that he would show up. I didn't believe him, but he was still invited, just like everyone else. As I pulled out of Teddy's in my silver Maserati (I've always loved cars) with my two friends, I immediately realized that I was in no condition to drive. But I was stubborn, and still peeled out onto Hollywood Blvd. After driving a little ways, I lost control of my car and crashed it into the center cement divider on the road. I even drove over the metal sign that warned you that the divider was approaching. Thank God no one was hurt, but my car was totaled. It was almost three in the morning, so when the LAPD pulled up and saw me sitting there—drunk but alive, with the front of my car folded inward and no other cars around—they already knew what had happened. They handcuffed me, and that's when I saw the paparazzi come charging at us. I started getting upset and threw the scarf that I had on over my head so no one could recognize me. Clearly that didn't work, and having a scarf over my head, standing next to a crashed car was like beckoning a crowd to form. The cops brought me over to the police station on Wilcox and put me in a holding cell. My cousin Takeya was staying with me at the time, so I used my one phone call and told her what was going on and to call my manager (Troy was still with me at this point) to get me out of there. As I'm explaining what happened and telling her I randomly invited everyone to my house, so she should be on the lookout, Takeya says to me, "Uh, there's some white dude already here sitting on the couch." I said, "Huh? Who?" She asked for his name, and in her very Philly way said to me, "Some Sean guy." It was Sean fucking Penn. Takeya had no idea who he was, which was kind of hilarious because she's totally unfazed by anything Hollywood ("He kind of looked familiar," she later told me). All she knew was that this older white gentleman was there for a party, apparently.

The whole situation sobered me up a little, but then panic set in when a visitor abruptly came to the police station. It was Sean Penn...again. He'd come to bail me out. Apparently, while he was waiting for me to get there for the after-party, Takeya told him I was in jail. And then there he was at the police station, ready to bail me out of there. I politely told him to leave, and he thought I was insane for doing that. But I wasn't too drunk to do the math, and if the paparazzi were already clocking me at the scene of the crime, then they most definitely were waiting outside the police station to find out what was gonna happen next. And if I walked outside with Sean Penn and everyone saw us, then the news headlines would be that we were together. It's not like his gesture wasn't kind, but the possible outcome was just too embarrassing for me to fathom. Imagine if I later had to explain in interviews that we weren't dating and that I'd just drunkenly invited an entire club to my home for a party? Nah. I was going through enough already. So I thanked him and sent him home. Troy posted the $30,000 bail instead.

I was charged with a DUI and later sentenced to probation, during which I had to attend AA meetings and wear an ankle monitor for fifty-six days. So in essence, I was forced into sobriety. Hollywood being *Hollywood* made it easier: I only had to attend a few AA meetings in person, and then someone came to my house instead. Even though I had the most LA experience with sobriety—where help comes to *you*—the thought of not being constantly drunk or high *terrified* me. I couldn't remember a time when I hadn't been drinking every single day. I pleaded to do community service instead. I offered to volunteer at hospitals, hospices, anywhere. I just couldn't imagine being sober for more than a few hours. Around the same time, I left Interscope (and parted ways with Troy), which was producing all sorts of emotions. I wanted to be numb, but by law I wasn't allowed to be.

Those fifty-six days saved my life.

I hadn't been sober in so long, and I hadn't really sat with my emotions in years. For the first time in a long time, I had to process what was going on in my life, and I had to deal with it all. So many thoughts and feelings flooded into my mind and I had to feel every last one of them. I briefly did therapy too, but also worked with a healer who helped

me unpack what I was going through. Once I'd done that,
I didn't want or need to feel numb anymore. I never had
some recovery story; I didn't even attend anything outside
of those AA meetings, unless I accompanied friends who
asked me to go with them. I have never really called that
time in my life a period of addiction, either, though I was
definitely headed in that direction. But once I learned how
to process my emotions and really take inventory of what
was happening, I didn't need to be mind-numbingly drunk
or high. That time slowed down my partying, but it also
gave me a moment to hit pause.

Right before I was sentenced to sobriety, though, another
incident happened that I think was the universe telling me
to slow down. I was in Las Vegas during the MTV VMAs,
and there was an after-party at one of the big-ass mansions
that used to be the hot spots to stay and party in while you
were there. It was my assistant's birthday, so I was trying to
get her a cake at the party, and I was running around the
place drinking, sometimes putting my drink down and picking it back up. It was an industry party, so I wasn't stressed
about my safety, really. I was amongst my peers—like, who
was gonna mess with me? I was drinking *a lot*, but the final
time I picked up my drink and took a sip, something felt off.
I was no stranger to drinking too much, but this was different. I felt out-of-body, like something was taking me over.
I realized that I had been drugged. Being aware of it actually caused me to start freaking out. I was sobbing uncontrollably. My security guard pulled me into a room, where
I was inconsolable. He saw me unable to calm down, and
said, "Okay, it's time to go." I said, "No wait! I feel crazy!"
I was screaming and saying, "Something's wrong with me."
Missy came in to check on me, but I was just unable to col-

lect myself. It was almost like my mind was fighting what was trying to get into my body. Just then, who walks in but Janet Jackson. I had never met her before, and so her first introduction to me was seeing me hysterical. I was embarrassed and still couldn't control myself. This was not how I wanted Janet fucking Jackson to meet me. None of that mattered to Janet; she actually just sprang into action and told people to get aspirin, water, hot sauce, and a piece of white bread. They brought it to her and she gave it to me, and that concoction knocked me right out of my hysteria. So basically Janet Jackson saved my life. Needless to say, though, that could have all been avoided if I hadn't been drinking so much and too drunk to realize that *nowhere* was safe enough to just put my drink down. I was ordered to start my fifty-six days soon after that incident.

After those fifty-six days, I was able to have a drink, but I was no longer in a constant state of chaos. I also learned how to manage my anxiety and face the next steps in my career head-on. I knew that I had to start taking meetings and, for the first time, begin the process of advocating for myself. That meant I had to have a clear head, which meant I had to be sober.

Over fifteen years later, I was feeding breakfast to my son, Wilde. I hadn't slept very well, but I'd still woken up feeling good—and was transported to the days when I never woke up feeling good. Back then, I would always feel like shit, and my solution would be to thug it out for a little while, before I would have some drinks to "balance it out." I sat in that moment in gratitude, thankful that those days were behind me, and I thanked God and my angels that I wasn't in that place anymore. And I will never return there again.

15

LIP LOCK

There I was, back as the only woman in a room full of men, rapping for my life again. I wasn't battling in the high school cafeteria this time; I wasn't at the Ruff Ryders studio in a cypher, either. The situation was familiar, yet the setting felt completely different. I was at a whole new record label, and I was trying to shop my next album. Alone.

My management situation was in a state of flux, where I tried out one manager, then joint managers, but no one seemed like the right connection. But I still had an album to sell, so it had to get done. I came to this one record label with a few finished songs. I was no stranger to anyone in the room, but that still didn't make the whole environment feel like it wasn't brand-new. Like *I* was brand-new. I sat down with everyone in the conference room, and I pressed Play. I started surveying their faces for a response, checking for head nods, you know the drill. I had never been by myself in a room full of executives before, but being an independent artist now, I had to do what I had to do. One exec in particular just looked totally disinterested. He started whispering to the other guys next to him, but you could tell they were trying to actually listen to my music—either out of courtesy or genuine interest. But that one dude, he was disengaged. He kept making eye contact with other men in the room and smirking, still whispering in ears, and then he started laughing. It wasn't like some full-on cackle, but the kind of cocky giggle where he wanted his bros to know he wasn't feeling it, and in turn neither should they.

I caught it all, and I was *not* gonna take that shit for one more minute. I had them stop the music, and I turned to the guy and looked him right in the eye. "Is there a problem?" I asked him. "Is there something funny? Is there a joke you wanna share?" You could tell he wasn't expecting me to ask him anything but permission to be in the room, but I was angry and had to speak. This wasn't just Philly Eve jumping out; this was an established artist demanding her respect. "Oh, nah. Nah," he replied to me, half nervous but not trying to show it. He gestured like his behavior wasn't a big deal and I was just getting upset for no reason. I believe we call that gaslighting. I knew his brother was a recording artist, and I wondered how he would've felt if his blood had come into a conference room to play his music and been laughed at. But that would never happen, would it? No man would dare whisper and giggle while another man was trying to play his music. It would be a series of exaggerated head nods and pounds at the end like he'd fuckin' just reinvented the wheel. I didn't expect a standing ovation, but I did expect some respect—but with no men around me to hype me up to the boys' club, I was just a woman to them. I wasn't an artist with a successful career and new music to share.

It wasn't just the men, either. I wanted the project to be professional, so I started taking meetings to look for a publicist. I was in the office of a well-known female publicist (my actual former publicist and a friend, I might add), and as I was explaining my vision for the publicity plan to her, she started ruffling through paperwork and took a damn phone call. Thank goodness that I got my poker face from my mom, because I literally had to keep my lips locked at that moment.

Shopping my fourth album was pure trauma, and it had a lot to do with finally entering those boardrooms that I hadn't been brought into as a signed artist. That's both a powerful and a weak position to be in. I lacked having an advocate with me, and when I would come with someone, it was usually just my tour manager/friendiger bestie Erin (I call her E-Lefty). But there's strength in your own advocacy, so I walked into those rooms knowing more than I ever had when I was signed. Also, I wasn't a new artist, and every executive in those rooms knew who I was. There were no introductions needed, but that didn't make the situation any easier for me. I quickly began to see just what goes down in those rooms, how you're not only at the mercy of the cliquey men inside them—you're also at the mercy of their hive mind. The biggest part of that collective mentality is keeping women in one box with their sound, for their own comfort. I wasn't going to go along with that. When I was recording my new project, I didn't want to stay in the same creative space I'd been in. So I kept experimenting with new sounds, something I tried to do with every project. That included trying different riffs on the guitar, and getting a whole piano into the studio to add to the musical experience. I was feeling a lot at the time, but mostly I wanted people to feel this album. And I took chances that I had never taken before. Now, I won't make any bold statements about how good the music was, but I will say that the things that I was doing on some of those songs later became a part of the hip-hop sound for men and women alike. I will definitely give myself credit for knowing what my own strengths were, and so I can't imagine everyone hating what I was doing with my music. But once you get into those meetings, you start feeling like that's exactly what was happening. Most of these guys can't see past the opinions of the man sitting next to them, though. It was that "all for one, one for all" game. There wasn't going to be that one guy to stand up and say, "All right, fuck it. Let's take a chance on this," even though in reality, it wasn't *that* much of a gamble. I was an artist with a proven track record. I had hits, many of which had come from me walking into the studio and saying, "Let's try this." Even when my label wasn't fully supporting me (like with "Tambourine"), I still had organic hits. So if my artistic intuition hadn't failed me then, why would it fail me now? Well, naturally, because there wasn't a man standing in the room with me to cosign it. Had there been, then there might have been a completely different outcome for *Lip Lock*.

When I first left Interscope, I was briefly signed to another label, and it felt like the politics game started all over again. I didn't last long there before I told myself that I had to leave to avoid making the same mistakes. So I was briefly signed and then back to being independent. Again. Because I was representing myself, the next step was showing up to labels with my new album and explaining how I wanted it to all go down.

It took a while to release *Lip Lock*. I was still busy with my film career and collaborating with other artists on their songs, but was still out there promoting my other music. I kept myself out there with remixes and freestyles (that I called EVEStylin), which kind of brought me into this mixtape era that I never had the chance to be a part of as a signed artist. Often that's the starting point for some, but here I was like reverse-engineering my career. *Lip Lock* would be the culmination of that, but I had to get in the right headspace first, which took some time. I wasn't numbing myself with anything, and I was making myself clear on how I wanted to handle my next project. I was fed up with simply being "signed" to a major label, and the next deal would have to work for me—my voice had to be heard and respect had to be given. Nobody wants to feel like a cash cow, and the difference here was that I no longer wanted to be one for somebody else's company. That's a harder ask for some of these men at the top, because they're surrendering complete ownership of you and your work in exchange for still accepting a financial risk. Not *every* meeting was terrible; some execs really loved me, but they just didn't know what to do with me. I wasn't anchored by the Ruff Ryders, so while they fucked with me, they didn't know how to approach my solo career. And with the music sounding so different than it had in the past, they weren't going to pull the trigger on some new shit with blind faith. Then there were some men who took it upon themselves to tell me that maybe I should go get married and have a baby instead (some of them even offered to be the father). Those were just more of the kinds of moments that you know would never happen to a man. Imagine telling some dude that instead of releasing his album, he should go find a wife and have kids? And while all of that just made me roll my eyes even harder, the attack on my music was what ultimately did me in. That one meeting with Mr. Giggles, that was my final straw. I couldn't put myself through that any longer. I wasn't going to keep shopping and keep shopping and hoping for a different outcome, when all it was doing was delaying the process for me. I've never been patient when it comes to my music.

So I stopped taking the meetings. I didn't want to put myself through the process of showing up for these men who were just waiting for the approval of the man next to them. That was the catalyst that led me to release *Lip Lock* all by myself. I finally had to say, "Fuck it. I'm going to do this. I'm going to make this album come out using my own money, even if I'm bone dead tired and ready to bang my head against a wall. And then those same guys who denied me are going to ask each other, 'How the hell did she do it?'" The hope for that end result became my fuel to release the album, even when I was running on fumes. The physical act of making and releasing music was exhausting me. I was so burned-out on the process before it even began. Mentally, I was still working on myself and physically I was maintaining a career that was in full swing. But I *hated* being underestimated, so I forced myself to finish that album. It became less about the music and more about proving to myself and the rest of the industry that I could put an album out on my own. I had to give myself that chance, and so I eventually secured a distribution deal with Sony Red and went to work on releasing my fourth album.

There were eleven years in between *Eve-Olution* and *Lip Lock*. In hip-hop years, that is an entire lifetime. I had lived so many different lives in between those two projects, so in coming back out, I can't say that I was my most confident self. *Lip Lock* was the first project where I worked with a few songwriters, which was an entirely new experience for me. I brought them on for a number of reasons. For one, I couldn't run my own little label (called From

The Rib), handle all the business matters, secure the distribution channels, and *then* write all the songs by myself. I
didn't have the bandwidth, and I needed that help. On top
of all that, I wasn't as creatively inspired to write the songs,
so I didn't even know how to just sit there and write my
thoughts down on my own like I had in the past. And as
much as I acted like the smirks and laughs from executives
didn't bother me, I started to question if my own songwriting abilities were the problem. Then I wondered if
this was still my chosen path or if I should pivot into something else. I had to quiet those emotions and just think of
ways to keep pushing ahead. Maybe I just needed to make
the music everyone else was making, or maybe my ideas
needed some help. There was a lot of self-doubt going on
in my mind at that time, so instead of giving up, I hired a
couple of writers to work with me—my cousin Takeya even
wrote on some stuff. I loved the art of collaboration anyway, along with switching genres and making music that
just sounded different. I also really wanted to make a more
musically inclined project, where I could do some of the
creative things that I never had the chance to when I was
signed, so this was my opportunity. The sacrifice was that
I was depending on myself less, which I honestly felt was a
lazier approach to making my music. It wasn't like I didn't
still have the heaviest hand in it when it came to writing
the songs, but just having more people involved made me
feel like I wasn't working as hard. Meanwhile, I was working the hardest I ever had in my life trying to put out this
project. I have a song on there called "Grind Or Die," and
I was definitely living by that mantra when I put this album
together. I was going through the motions, really, just to get
this album out. But I was stressed. Life was stressful. I *was*
the label now, financing the whole operation. In the midst

of it all, life was in limbo. While I was still making money, it wasn't like the money I had made before, so I had to sell my house in LA (which I'd loved) for a cheaper price and move back to New York City. I had to sell my art, including this one Andy Warhol painting that I absolutely loved, to make money. It was devastating for me and felt horrible, but I knew that I would make it out on the other side.

At my core, though, I was a successful artist now facing the fact that I was on my own, asking myself if I could do this again. Could I be successful on my own, without my past label, and without the Ruff Ryders? I was trying to process it all as the losses piled on, all while trying to make this album happen.

Lip Lock was totally grassroots, and while I didn't feel like I was able to put all of myself into it musically (not while balancing the business side of it all), I still call it my most "musical" album. I sort of had a manager (who wound up being the wrong fit for me) and I had my lawyer, who I did lean heavily upon. They both made some suggestions about the kind of team that I needed to hire in order to make this work. The goal was to bring on people who could handle those things that I was missing without a label behind me. I then took meetings with some people and assembled a team of individuals who were still in the thick of it, industry-wise. They had connections to the radio stations and all of the key people there, worked with major labels on the side, had key contacts at venues, knew about budgeting, and just had a good lay of the land. It was definitely trial and error with those meetings, though. I would talk to some people and see if they were a good fit. If they were, then it was "welcome to the team." If they weren't, then I'd move onto the next person. I had my bestie Erin working with me too, as well as our amazing assistant Binta, and I

had a small office setup. It really was like its own little record label, with a support staff and everything. I was very
fortunate to end up with a group of people who were on
board and invested in the project. It was a small team, yet
a dedicated one. They didn't come at the behest of a record
label; they were there for me and my vision.

I also had musicians who showed up for me, no questions asked. Producers like Salaam Remi came on board for
my song "Forgive Me," and I really appreciated how much
he understood where I was going with *Lip Lock*. That's
because he's a real artist. I relied heavily on my cowriter
Nicholas Oshane Moore (I called him Shane), who really
helped me through the songwriting process. I also worked
with producers like Radio8, Jukebox, Jon Jon, Blac Elvis,
Felix Snow, and Sander Van Der Waal—musicians who I
may have never had an opportunity to collaborate with if
there was still a major label in charge. Swizz even worked
with me on "Mama in the Kitchen," and I had Snoop Dogg
featured on that track. That was another part of the process that I was so grateful for. Whether it was Snoop Dogg
or Missy Elliott, Juicy J, Pusha T, any of the artists I collaborated with on the album…they were there for me and
wanted to be a part of the project. That meant so much,
because it was a different kind of album than they were
used to hearing from me, and yet they still came on board
on the strength of wanting to work with me. That same
love carried over into radio, where my singles were played
by DJs who really just loved and supported me. I appreciated that as well. Back then, it was different; there were a
limited number of channels to promote your music. Today,
there are so many avenues for your music to find its audience. And since I didn't have a label, I was never going to
"compete" with those who did. I had to rely on my repu-

tation, the relationships that I'd built, and the quality of the music that I was known for bringing.

This wasn't going to be an "industry" album, no matter what. I'd reached this point in my career where I wasn't going to just cater to the singles rinse cycle and churn out songs for the radio. Sure, I could have something on there for people to shake their asses to, but I had to have more meaning behind the music or else I was just going to check out all over again. I also couldn't just make some traditional rap records. I needed those different sounds, I needed those different genres, I needed to rap at different tempos, and I needed to sing when I wanted to. For the first time, I brought live instruments into the studio too. I was in a different stage of my life and the music had to show all of that. I was also working with Big Brothers Big Sisters of America at the time, and we brought one of the album's songs ("Make It Out This Town" with Gabe Saporta from the pop/EDM group Cobra Starship) into their marketing campaign. I got some hate for working with Gabe—not because of any Cobra Starship shade, but because people didn't understand why I was going in that direction. In reality, it was actually really organic. I went to a Cobra Starship concert, I met Gabe, and we decided to make a positive record together that spoke to the philanthropy stuff that I was doing on the side. There wasn't much more to it than that.

I funded everything for *Lip Lock* on my own—from the music videos for my singles ("Eve," "She Bad Bad," and "Make It Out This Town"), to the radio promo tour, to the actual album tour, to the team helping me put it all together. I had no major label support, and there were times when I really, really felt that lack of backing. You don't know what you have until it's gone, but in its place I had a freedom that I'd never had before. It took so much work to put that album out, and I was doing things for the first time that I had never done in all of my years as a recording artist. I was in a van touring the country, doing shows at smaller venues. I was moving through cities like an artist on Day One of the job. But all of that excited me. I never had that opportunity before. I became a stadium star so quickly that I never got to be that up-and-coming artist, performing at small clubs and getting that "indie" moment. What that also entailed was playing in different venues that I would have never gotten to play in had I still been signed to a major label. I remember being able to perform at the Roxy on Hollywood Boulevard, knowing that Bob Marley had once played there. Talk about legendary. That felt so cool to me. It felt real. It felt tangible. I was in an era of my music career when I could experience things I hadn't before, which for me was like being the rap equivalent of an alt-girl or a rising grunge star, like I was in the early days of Nirvana. And I really embraced it. The sound on *Lip Lock* also reflected that. The truth was, this was the album that I'd been trying to make when I was signed, but everyone kept pushing back on it. This was my opportunity to get it out of my system.

As I listen to *Lip Lock* now, I'm so proud of myself for doing it. The critics liked it too—one even suggested that it should've been the album titled *Eve-Olution* since I was being more "adventurous." People genuinely felt my honesty. I spent more money than I made (yet again), but it was worth it. *Lip Lock* was a lot of work, though, and took more time than ever to record, release, and promote it.

But at least I can say that I did it.

16

MAXIMILLION

It's almost midnight, and I'm sitting alone in a room at one of the smaller, more secluded Canadian border crossings in the backwoods of Vermont, and the border patrol thinks I'm a drug mule.

At least that's how it looks. I mean, I showed up in a drop-top Bentley Continental with Florida license plates and two blonde girls. We didn't look shady at all. There were only two guards on duty, and they had no computers to even scan our passports and register who we were at their location.

That was the whole point.

When the opportunity to ride in the Gumball 3000 rally came to me through a friend who worked in fashion, I was all-in. The Gumball 3000 rally is basically a rolling festival where car enthusiasts come together every summer and drive (not race) three thousand miles across different locations around the world. It's like summer camp for people who love cars and adventure. I've always loved both, so the idea of driving three thousand miles over seven days in a supercar was so exciting. Plus, the 2010 rally started in London and jumped across the pond to end in New York. How cool is that?

I've always had this suspicion that all British men think that they're James Bond, though once I met Maximillion Cooper, I kind of believed that he might be. Max founded Gumball in 1999 and had been doing these annual rallies ever since. It was supposed to be a smooth ride, metaphorically and physically, but that came to an end when I was stopped at the American border heading into Quebec. It was all thanks to my damn DUI from three years earlier. When traveling to either Canada and Australia, I had to come with a letter attached to my passport, acknowledging my DUI and showing that my charges were expunged, which would grant me access into the country. To this day, I still need to show a current letter when I reach Canada or Australia. After my Teddy's incident, I had received that letter acknowledging my expungement, but it had expired, so when I first tried to get into Canada at a larger border crossing, my passport scan reflected that I had a DUI and I was pulled over by the patrol. I was in the car with Erin and our friend who brought me into the rally as we watched every other car in the Gumball car line peal past us.

When Max approached the border, he saw us stranded there and pulled over. He asked the guards what the problem was, and they told him that I wasn't allowed into the country because I had a DUI and an expired letter. How embarrassing. Max attempted to vouch for me, but they didn't want to hear any part of it. A sheik from Saudi Arabia who was participating in the rally even pulled over and attempted to help. Didn't work. I was getting upset and anxious, but, maintaining what I later learned was his usual demeanor, Max was pretty calm, cool, and collected.

He then called the chief of police in Quebec. "How does he even know all of these people?" I thought. He came back to my car and said, "Okay, you're going to have to go a different way. I'm gonna find you the route." It required using a map. A *physical* map. But since this particular border crossing was small and buried deep in the woods of Vermont, it had no computers to scan my passport with. That meant that they couldn't register my DUI or the letter that was supposed to be attached. I was basically sneaking into Canada. We had to remove all the Gumball wrappings off the car and head through this forest. When we finally got to that smaller stop, the border patrol looked at the three of us in this expensive car and were like, "What the hell is going on here?" and made us get out of the car. Great.

The guards split us up into separate rooms. "Where are you girls going?" the one guard asked me. "Are you driving in the Gumball rally?" I pretended not to know what the hell he was talking about. "Uh, *no!*" I replied. "We do this college road trip like *every year!*" The guard looked at my wrist, and I realized I was still wearing a Gumball 3000 bracelet. I'd forgotten to take that off. Whoops. "Well, what's *that?*" he said, pointing to my bracelet. "Oh *that!*" I replied. "Well, they were throwing those things out the window, so you know, we just found them and put them on." Somehow they bought it and allowed us through. I called Max and told him what'd happened, and he said to just keep driving.

As we crossed the border in torrential rain at nearly three

o'clock in the morning, the first person I saw on the other side was Max. My James Bond. He was smiling, knowing he had basically done the impossible, as I thought to my-self, *"Who are you?"*

Before Max and I met, I decided that my casual dating days were over. For years, I had been on this roller coaster ride of connections that lacked any real meaning for me. I moved like a guy, which you could call the result of trauma from my past relationships, but which I call emotional sur-vival. It was tiring trying to make relationships out of sit-uations that were never going to be significant to begin with. I hit a wall, though, and had just had enough, and I made the decision that my next relationship would have to be something serious; otherwise, I didn't want it. I wasn't looking, but I also didn't have any care to *be* looking, any-way. When I say I was done, I was *done.*

Meanwhile, Max thought his dating days were just start-ing. He was newly divorced after nearly eight years of mar-riage. He really thought he was stepping into his "player" era, and a new commitment was the furthest thing from his mind.

Then we met, and it was game over for the both of us.

As someone who was wallowing in my own apathy when it came to dating, I was confused by Maximillion Coo-per. I automatically cared too much about him. We'd met when I landed in London for the first part of the Gum-ball rally, and for some reason he intrigued me. I wanted to know *everything* about him. That annoyed the shit out of me, because I was fully prepared to not care about him or any other man. But there was a connection, one that I kept trying to deny. The rally was only one week long, but a lot can happen in seven days—and it did. I fully expected to never see him again afterward, though, even after he rescued me at the border. After all, he lived in London, I lived in Los Angeles, and I was in my "I don't care" mode. That didn't stop me from continuing to think about him as I boarded my flight back to LA, though.

A few days after I returned home from Gumball, Max called me. "I'm coming to LA this weekend," he said. I was like, "Why?" He said, "To see you." I was a little shocked. "Really?" I replied. Then he said something that no other man had ever said to me before. He said, "Look, I don't know what this is or where it's gonna go. It might not go anywhere, but I don't want to risk losing this connection." It was direct and honest. No games. Before that moment, I had told a friend of mine that the only way the next man was going to win me over was if he came and got me.

And Max came and got me.

I made the decision to take a chance. We were both grown and nobody was demanding marriage or anything. If the relationship worked out, then it worked out. If it didn't, then it didn't. Again, my interest in dating in general was already low at the time, so the risk seemed much lower than the possible reward. So I told him he could come see me in LA that weekend on one condition: he had to babysit my dogs.

I was traveling to Detroit for a show at a casino and let him stay at my place in LA while I was gone. When I got back, we had two days together. Our first date was at my favorite taco spot, Pinches Tacos. In those two days, I realized the connection with Max was different. It was intense—it was honest. We didn't show up like it was a fling; we had an open conversation about where we were at in our lives. And even though we thought we had our own plans for ourselves in place, I guess the universe had a dif-

ferent plan for the both of us. So I went with it, and so did
he, and I kind of let my heart guide me. I think the reason
why it worked for us was because we talked *so much*. It's all
we had, really, being so long-distance. We were still using
Blackberries and had these lengthy conversations like five
times a day. It was the most I had ever spoken to another
human being in my entire life. There was constant com-
munication, enough to really speed up getting to know
someone. This wasn't just a series of casual dates. We didn't
have that luxury. These were just continuous and very open
conversations. When we did meet up, it was in different
cities across the world for romantic weekends. But when
you're that connected to someone, those moments aren't
nearly enough. We hit a point where we both knew this was
getting serious. I found myself in London more; I would
perform somewhere in Europe like Germany or Italy and
then head over to Max for a week or two in London before heading back to LA. Once I started working on *Lip
Lock*, I made the decision to move to New York to record
it, but also to be closer to London to see him more. That
made things slightly easier, but again it just wasn't enough.
Our relationship was getting too serious.

I think about the timing of it all now and how the physical distance actually saved us in the beginning. We were
both works in progress. Max had four kids, and two of them
were super young. He'd been married for so long, was newly
divorced, and going through emotions as well. He carried a
lot of baggage, but then again so did I. I was unlearning so
much about relationships, from my past experiences. Had
we coexisted in the same city while trying to figure this
out, then maybe it wouldn't have worked at all. We might
have even rushed into something very serious, which could

have snowballed. Instead, we had these sporadic but important times together. If I was in Italy or something and he'd come meet me there, it would be for a brief romantic getaway in between these constant conversations we were having. It allowed us to bypass dumping the heavier parts of what we were both dealing with onto each other. The thing about baggage is that you have to unpack it, and that's exactly what we did…on our own, before we ended up together. It wasn't easy, but most worthwhile things aren't.

Still, we did reach this point where the next level was staring at us, but we were also at a crossroads. We could continue down this path of long-distance, but eventually something would have to give. One of us had to be the person to ultimately uproot their lives in the long run for the sake of the other person. Someone had to make that compromise. That someone was me. In order to really make this work, I had to do something that I'd been extremely uncomfortable doing in my past relationships: I had to relinquish control. I had to jump in with both feet, but with my eyes wide open. Max had kids back home in England, so there was no way he could be with me with any consistency. I had to be over there more for this to work, and to even know if there was a real future for us. Once I'd finished recording *Lip Lock* and released it, there was nothing really holding me back. And even with recording, I could do that anywhere. I was already performing in Europe regularly. What difference did any of that *really* make? So I made the decision to spend most of my time in London after that.

When I first told Erin, the first thing she said to me was, "I can't believe that you're going to do all of that without a ring." My response to her was like, "Look, I'm doing this to see if I *want* the ring." It wasn't like I was going to be forcibly planted in London and couldn't go right back to the States when I wanted to. The truth of the matter was that I *always* felt like I was going to one day live in Europe. Whether it was London or Paris, when I first started my career and traveled to these places and experienced the pacing of the lives over there, I wanted that. I never wanted to be in the rat race permanently, and for me things always felt different when I was in Europe. So while the decision involved the biggest adjustment to my own ego in the relationship, I already loved where I was headed.

And most of all, I loved the person I was heading there with.

Max and I spent years dating, as most of my time was spent in London with him. Prior to that point, we hadn't spent significant time together in any one place. The idea of seriously considering marriage didn't even enter the picture until right before it happened. That's because we made the decision that if and when we got engaged, the wedding would happen within six months. It wasn't going to be a situation where we would be engaged for years. That would have made no sense at all. What's the point then? So on December 25, 2013, Max and I got engaged. Six months later, on June 14, 2014, we were married, and I became a London resident for good.

Those years of dating while being in the same location helped us out a lot. London isn't exactly the same as the United States, culturally, but at least I wasn't learning an entirely new language or anything—it was more a matter of understanding my new city and all of the customs that came with it. I was also in a city that I actually already loved, so that made it much easier. When I first started spending more time in London, I was overwhelmed at the idea of Max having four children. I didn't know if that was something that I was prepared to take on full-time, or something that I even wanted for myself. But very early on, Max made his children a part of our relationship. He didn't separate his life in two like some people do when they start dating after a divorce. I met him as an incredible father who loved his children, and in turn, I loved them too. But before spending any real time with them, I hadn't been around kids in so long. I didn't even know how to talk to children. I didn't know anything about homework, or dropping kids off at school, or picking them up at the end of the day—basically, centering your entire schedule around theirs—but I learned to really enjoy the parts of our relationship where the kids were involved. It probably took me a solid two years or so to really get the hang of all that, but I learned how to handle it before becoming his wife and their stepmom. After all that time together, they aren't my "stepkids" to me; they are my "bonus kids."

There were other parts of our pre-married life together that also required some adjusting. I wouldn't say Max "adulted" more than I did, but our lives moved at different paces, something neither of us really understood when our relationship lived over Blackberry messages. I was still traveling a lot to tour, doing club dates in different cities across Europe—but then coming "home" to Max as opposed to him meeting me at my hotel in whatever city, which was much different. Now if I did a show in Germany or Italy, I'd be heading back to London for family time after. There were times when I'd have been up super late from performing the night before, after a full weekend of back-to-back shows, and then heading back to London.

When I got there, Max would say, "Okay, we are heading to the countryside with the kids to see my parents for two days," and I'd be like, "Wait, are you serious?" I was promoting an album, and he was being a present parent. Both are important jobs, but neither look the same. Both can be fulfilling, but both can be exhausting. I had to learn how to balance the two, but Max and I also had to learn how to coexist in each other's lives. Before being with him, my holidays were spent on vacation—you could find me on an island in the Caribbean during Christmas—but that all changed. Holidays were spent with family. His kids are also very affectionate. They hug, they say "I love you" a lot. I wasn't raised that way, so I acclimated, and I'm happy that I did.

I have been blessed with amazing in-laws and bonus kids, but in the beginning, none of them really understood what I did for a living. Sure, they might have known who I was, but what you see on television is different from what you're living day-to-day. Max and I were totally different; we didn't have a lot in common outside of some shared interests, like our mutual love of travel. The thing that really connected us was how we were both self-made and understood the value of work. But it's like, how do you even learn to move as a unit? I had also never really seriously dated a white guy before, and Max had never dated a Black woman. He had to learn about things, even like how I did my hair. We had to learn to have open conversations about race, about politics. But the optics of our being together was more so an adjustment for the people around us, especially in the beginning.

I remember when I first started bringing Max around to my friends in hip-hop, there were some…mixed reviews.

Everybody was shocked that this was the guy I was dating. One of my close guy friends in the game said to me, "Yeah, he's cool. Don't marry that white guy, though." He meant it too. He sincerely didn't want me to end up with a white dude. It looked "new" to hip-hop for me to be showing up with someone who was white, especially when in the rap game it was just like everyone was dating each other. So when I took myself out of that pool, there was pushback. I get it, but that wasn't something I was going to make a deal breaker for me and my happiness. Both Max and I would get DMs on our Instagram accounts with some strong opinions about us dating. Once people saw that we were serious, I guess they kind of gave up on fighting us. It was something that I had to take stock of, though. Like, *when* do I bring this man around? How *often* should I bring him? While I wasn't really super tight with the Ruff Ryders by the time I released *Lip Lock*, they all met him at that album release party in New York City for the first time. They were all confused. It was like my worlds were colliding.

In the end, though, the biggest adjustment was to what was going on in my own mind, and that's still a work in progress. My first real relationship burned me, and any man who followed had to pay the price until I met Max. That was because he understood he had to prove his loyalty, since it had never been given to me freely by any man in my life before him. He already knew how to be married and how to be a husband and father (which also helped), but even before we were married, he kind of knew how to talk to me when I was spiraling. I was always in fight mode, fiercely independent, and he showed me that I could lean on someone—that we could lean on each other. He was patient with me while I learned how to trust a man in my life. It was so hard at the start, when I was living in Los Angeles and he was in London. Sometimes the time difference led to missed calls, and I would automatically assume he wasn't taking us seriously, when he was really just asleep because it was 4:00 a.m. for him and not 8:00 p.m. like where I was. My past relationship trauma would pop right back up. It led to me saying things like, "Okay, so I guess we're over now. Fuck this." He wouldn't let me do that to us, but he also knew where it was coming from. He had to finally stop me and say, "I am *not* that guy," and I had to believe him.

The odds were kind of against us, given all of the circumstances, but we fought to make it work. And once we found our groove, it just made sense. I did find it ironic, though, how the world decided that I became a kept woman once Max and I got together—like I didn't have a massive career before meeting him, like we weren't both self-made millionaires. It stung, especially when I was continuing to work successfully in my career. We help *each other* out. We take *each other* on vacations. We throw *each other* parties. There's just something about the built-in biases when it comes to gender and success that never has and never will sit right with me. Even when Max and I are out at places like a hotel or a nice restaurant and I'm the one paying, they'll address him like he's the person footing the bill. That's more of a society issue, though, and not specific to two successful public figures in a marriage. But if the world chooses to focus on my "soft life," then so be it. I'd rather that than the anxiety-filled "hard life" that I'd lived before.

I will tell you this much, though: Maximillion Cooper is my biggest fan.

He is so happy at my shows. He walks around and greets people, passing around drinks like he's the host. I tell him he's corny, but it's honestly so sweet and adorable. I'd never had a man by my side who supports me the way he does. I'd had men who wanted to *compete* with me, or who got upset when my career was lapping theirs. Those relationships were built on jealousy and their hope that they would always be ahead of me somehow. It isn't like that with Max. He really loves my career because he knows how much *I* love it. In turn, I wave the flag hard for Gumball 3000. I am so proud when I see Max at his rallies, how hard he works on his brand even in between those moments. How he's brought so many people together, from so many different cultures, in so many different corners of the world. How he has traveled to otherwise impossible-to-visit places like North Korea on the strength of his passion, his personality, and his heart. I also love performing at his Gumball after-parties, celebrating him and the place where I met the man I was meant to end up with. Max built his empire on his own, just like I did with mine, and so we show up for each other and honor that.

I believe you call that a power couple.

17

ACT TWO

Blood was pouring out of my nose like a faucet. I had never been punched in the face like that before, and definitely not by a man. My eyes were tearing up, and I was in so much pain that I couldn't breathe. The people around us rushed over and tried to stop everything, but I told them not to.

"Just keep rolling," I said.

I was in Cape Town for two weeks, filming an independent movie with Daniel Craig called *Flashbacks of a Fool*. In it, I play Daniel's character's assistant, and in one scene, while I'm attempting to put his dog in a car, he accidentally punches me in the face. Then two women come up to help me, and I flip out on *them* instead. As we were shooting the scene, the dog started wiggling in my arms, causing Daniel to actually punch me dead in the nose. It was a total accident, but needless to say I was caught off guard. After it happened, the director wanted to end the day and get me to the hospital since I was very obviously injured, but I refused. I was in so much pain, I was bleeding, my eyes were watering, and I was mad. But I knew that I would *never* act as well as I would in that moment. I would never actually be that angry or in agony without that physical impact (not to mention my real blood being all over me). If I'd waited until the next day, I'd have been on painkillers and would have already processed the moment. The swelling would have gone down, and the moment would've been lost. I'm an actor, so I wanted to keep acting in that scene with as much authenticity as possible. They should use the pain, use the emotions, and hell, use the physical trauma. So, through gritted teeth, I told them to keep the cameras rolling, and they did. Later that night, Daniel had a magnum of vodka sent to my hotel, with a note that said, "First of all, I am so sorry. Second of all, you are a fucking pro."

Whether it was *Whip It* or *Glee*, and everywhere in between, film and TV sets became the equivalent of concert stages for me, and so I took them all just as seriously. They were places where I wanted to perform to the absolute best of my ability, never compromising quality.

Filming *Barbershop* was no different, and it was my most consistent experience outside of my own TV show. It took a while to figure all of that out, since I was still partying while trying to film *Eve* and *Barbershop* almost simultaneously. For the first *Barbershop*, I was on hiatus from my *Eve* series, so I basically just moved to Chicago, where we filmed that first movie. It was cold as hell when we filmed, but that didn't stop me from going out and drinking way more than I should have when I'd have to film the next day. I don't know how I still managed to function for like a sixteen-hour shoot after a night of partying, but I'm gonna give all the credit to youth for that. You can't catch me in that cycle now, though.

By *Barbershop 2: Back in Business*, I was commuting back and forth from LA to film in Chicago, while still doing my music stuff all throughout. The thing that was missing for me was having any rituals to keep myself together, but at that point I didn't even know I needed any of that. Still, I really loved being on set. The cast was cool, I loved my role, and we built a sense of community on set, the crew included. That made me appreciate the experience even more.

That franchise had me grow with my character Terri across two films, though by the third one I wasn't sure why it was still happening. It had been well over ten years since the first two films were released. Why couldn't we just leave well enough alone? When I found out *Barbershop: The Next Cut* was greenlit, though, I was still going to come on board, especially after I read the script. Terri's character was going to have more dimensions, and there was more depth to where she was going in her life, her career, and her marriage. At that point, I had to say yes. I wasn't gonna do Terri like that; I had to round out her storyline in the trilogy for the character's sake. I knew that another female rapper was going to join the cast, but initially I wasn't made aware of who it was. Obviously the writers and the director of the film knew, and I later learned that my agents did too. They all kept that information from me, as if I somehow couldn't handle the news. I found out from some other random person who my costar was going to be.

It was Nicki Minaj.

Once I heard that, there was something I felt like I had to do: I put myself into therapy.

The idea of being on set with Nicki Minaj just brought me so much anxiety. That's why I decided to seek some help to get stronger for that moment. It was for my own survival, really. I've lived through what happens when women project their own insecurities onto other women. It happened at the start of my career and continued in waves as my fame grew. I wasn't going to be that woman to someone else, but in order to do that, I had to physically and mentally prepare myself.

In the months leading up to filming, I started eating clean, exercising more, and getting mindful again. By then, I knew what anxiety was, and I knew that I was prone to being overcome by it, so my course of action was to cut it off before it got so bad that I couldn't function. It was like I was preparing for my own internal disaster, like I wasn't going to be able to handle what was about to happen on set. It bothered me that my own team felt the same way, and that I had already been conditioned in my own mind to agree with them. Since I was kind of in the thick of my own spiritual journey, I sought out this therapist who also worked as a healer. I didn't want to just recognize my anxiety—I also wanted to figure out what it was bringing up inside of me. It wasn't exactly *fear*, but more not wanting to feel thrown away or disregarded, like I had felt about my record label in the past. I also didn't want that to derail me and the progress that I had made.

My state of mind was so different back during the making of the first two films. I thought that I was invincible and could lead so many lives—both on and off camera—in one body. I was doing too much, so the one promise that I did make to myself (even before I knew who my costar was) involved reversing all of the habits that I first came on set with as a twenty-four-year-old. This switch was inspired by my own life change. I was the catalyst, but everything that followed only added to the need for it.

I couldn't help but feel like this was a monumental moment, like a changing of the guard, and one that I'd never really anticipated happening on set. Through both *Barbershop* and *Barbershop 2: Back in Business*, I was *that* chick. I was *EVE*, the female rap star delegate in an ensemble cast, at the height of her rap career. Even when Queen Latifah came on board for the sequel, it was a different scenario because she was already a Hollywood legend and my position as the female rap star in the cast was still fixed in place. And even though I did put my all into the Terri Jones character, there was still a level of stardom that came with me simply by existing. So no matter what, my presence came with all of the bells and whistles on set. I was *always* a team player, though, through and through, and I was always nice to people. I still try my best to remain a kind and gracious professional in any environment. They did consider me a big deal, though. It was reflected in the promotion of the film, right down to how I was top billed in the credits. On the posters, I was set apart from the guys; it was all very intentional marketing. That all changed when Nicki came on board. By that point, she was leading the new charge for rap royalty, and getting her in the film felt like a big win for the team. Their excitement was palpable. I should know, because I was in her position once.

Five years before we filmed the third *Barbershop*, I was standing on a music video set with a still-new Nicki Minaj. She was only a few years out from her mixtape era, and was just getting ready to release her debut album, *Pink Friday*. We met as she was on the verge of her greatness, while I was already well settled into mine. Our paths crossed for the first time on the remix to Ludacris's "My Chick Bad"— the original single featured Nicki. She was also front and center in the song's music video. The remix had Diamond from Crime Mob, Trina, and then me on cleanup, which in rap lingo means they've saved the best for last. We shot the music video the same day as Nicki's video shoot (she wasn't featured on the remix), but during the filming for our video, she was bumped to the back. There was no doubt that Nicki was on the come-up at that point, but in that environment, I was still the "it" girl. You can even see Nicki dancing in the background as we're spitting our verses in the video.

Now here I am, back on the *Barbershop* set years later, and the tables have turned. Nicki is the "it" girl, and I was bumped down. It was a shock, but something I knew was bound to happen, given how women in rap are handled. We can tell ourselves all day that the motto "there can only be one" is fake, but when it plays out in real life, you see how the outside world still abides by it. The crew didn't hide that fact, either. When I was emailed about the credits in the film, it was like they were trying to buffer me and somehow protect me from disappointment. The emails said something to the effect of "We can't give you the top-billed credit that we once did," which was within the first four names billed. Whatever. It didn't faze me, honestly. And even after they decided to send that email to me, they still billed me the way that I always had been (though Nicki had her own special credit at the end).

Even though Terri's story arc had evolved, and there was a stronger narrative for her—one that really had Nicki playing a secondary role—I was still not the priority cast mem-

ber that I had once been. You even saw it on the movie
poster, where Nicki is positioned up front, just as I had been
on the previous posters. She had her own bus, her own hair
and makeup team, everything. So did I at one point. It was
all just different now, and it felt...weird. Like I was just a
part of the cast and she was the guest of honor. But I had
braced myself for it and taken all of the measures I needed
to in order to get myself ready for this moment. I was not
going to look like the disgruntled girl on set, sizing myself
up to the new chick while the men stood around us to see
what would happen next, observing our dynamic, waiting
for some catfight. No way in hell. It wasn't happening. I'd
also assumed that I was going to care way more than I actually did once everything started playing out.

On set, the crew didn't know how to speak "rapper" and
attempted to come to me for all of their Nicki Minaj needs.
Meanwhile Ice Cube, Common *and* Tyga are literally *right
there*. I wasn't gonna be the Hip-Hop Den Mother. No
thanks. I politely told them that I wasn't doing anything
other than acting without a producer credit. That wasn't
me being petty, either. I just wasn't willing to do more for
them than they were doing for me. Also, I was in a place
of healing in my life, and I just couldn't let something that
I once loved make me feel anything but peace. I had been
down that road so many times. And so I did something
about it. I talked it out in therapy, I recited mantras when I
woke up, and I meditated daily. I didn't drink at all, because
I started to realize that *all* of that "fun" shows up on camera,
especially as you get older. I also committed to an intense
two-a-day workout regimen. I love my castmate Regina
Hall so much, especially since she and I really teamed up
and worked out after filming every night. We'd wrap at

like midnight or 1:00 a.m. and then go and get in another thirty or forty minutes down at the gym. Basically, I was putting myself in a position to be completely disciplined, mentally, physically, and emotionally.

All of this had nothing to do with Nicki, really. It wasn't like I was over in the gym doing squats just to stand next to her or reciting mantras to avoid a meltdown in her presence. This had more to do with me and less to do with her. Really, it had more to do with what she represented, which was an acknowledgment that I was at a different level in my life now. My therapist told me (and I still have the paper I wrote it all down on) that this was just a shift in my life. There was nothing wrong with that or wrong with me; I was just evolving. When we started filming, I was two years into marriage and living in London. I had to temporarily relocate to Atlanta for three months to film the movie. I was in such a different stage in my life. I was happy, still working, but not searching to figure myself out. I had to learn to separate myself emotionally from the situation and just kind of almost watch myself in the moment, while reminding myself that I was in such a better place in my life.

But those old feelings did temporarily come flooding back when I first heard that Nicki Minaj was going to be in the film. That's what the industry does to women sometimes. It makes us feel bad about ourselves and our positions, and it makes us feel replaceable. In my mind, the writers didn't see it as adding to the ensemble cast—they saw it as "Eve has now been replaced by Nicki Minaj." I doubt Ice Cube felt that way about Common, but it's something that we as women have to sit with in every stage of our careers. It's how we quietly get pitted against each other, right down to everyone withholding the information that Nicki was going to be in the film out of fear that I would have turned it down. This was not the first or the last time that a woman would be duped into showing up to some shit without the full lay of the land, and then everyone acts surprised when emotions run high. You can't cause tension and then wonder why everyone is tense. That's not how it works. Nicki and I were actually fine on set. We got along well and shot our scenes together with no problems. It was nothing like what I had expected, but again, I am thankful that I prepared myself for it.

Nicki's schedule started to get busier, so she wrapped on set before the rest of us, but once we did, I gave myself some time to have fun. During that period, it felt like *everyone* was filming in Atlanta, including the cast of *Captain America*. We were all staying at the same hotel, and after wrapping I went down to the bar to have a drink (I allowed myself after that), and who came down but Captain America himself, Chris Evans, and Anthony Mackie, who I call Black Captain America. It was me and a couple of my other castmates with those guys. Chris had this sick-ass penthouse suite at the hotel. It was like an apartment! We all went up to hang out, but then they asked us what we were doing next. I said, "Well, I'm trying to go to Magic City," because hello, lemon pepper wings. I ended up bringing Chris Evans, aka Captain America, to the infamous strip club Magic City. He was so uncomfortable, because he's just so sweet and polite, but I was the one to bring him to Magic City for the first time. It was a cool way to finish my time shooting *Barbershop: The Next Cut* and really closing out that chapter in my career. Even though it felt like a rocky start, there was really nothing rocky about it.

There was one moment during filming, though, that I think was the epiphany for me, and that was watching how hard Nicki had to work as a rapper while still learning the ropes of being an actor. She didn't know that we did all of our hair and makeup together or that we all ate lunch together. There's a communal vibe on set, one that I had to learn too, so I understood when she hadn't yet gotten the hang of it. Plus, Nicki really was the "it" girl, and with that comes a lot of shit. So I'd see her writing songs on her bus in between takes, hurrying off set to go hit some show dates over the weekend and then come right back on set for these twelve-to-sixteen-hour shoots, all while trying to hold together her personal life and her relationship. It was at that moment that I didn't envy her, and I kind of wanted to give her a hug. I thought I was going to resent her, and really all I felt was compassion. I remembered being that person, the girl who felt like she had to do it all. The girl who was pressured to do it all, because it was all eyes on her. Instead of feeling insecure around Nicki, I started to sympathize with her. I was so thankful that I had left that part of my life behind—I was glad to be done with it. I think at the heart of it, though, *Barbershop* was a life test for me that I am proud to say I passed. The universe was asking me, "Have you really changed?" and my response was, "Yes. I have."

18

LET'S TALK ABOUT IT

I'd only been a part of *The Talk* for three days when I knew I wanted to quit that talk show for good. In that short time frame, I had experienced something that had never happened to me before.

I was doxed.

It happened right after I gave my thoughts on air about Nicki Minaj's *PAPER* Magazine cover for their Winter 2017 issue. On it, there are three different versions of Nicki; one is sitting in a chair topless and the other two are touching her. *PAPER* was known for their #breaktheinternet magazine covers. This was the same magazine that had Kim Kardashian with her bare butt out. I get the shock value of it all, even if it's not my thing. My cohosts asked for my opinion on Nicki's cover, and so I told them. It had been well over a year since we were in *Barbershop: The Next Cut*, and while I had respect for her as a lyricist and as a person (and I said that on air), I just didn't think that the cover was the best idea. I mean, it's how I felt, and I was speaking about it like rapper to rapper, female celeb to female celeb. That's basically why my cohosts even asked for my hot take on it. My standpoint was pretty clear: I explained that I had reached a point in my own rap career where I recognized that girls were looking up to me, and that I hoped Nicki realized that for herself and her fans too. I wasn't judging her at all. It wasn't like I was acting horrified by her photo; I just basically expressed that it was not for me. It was no disrespect to Nicki Minaj.

Her fans felt otherwise.

As soon as the video clip from our show circulated on the internet, so did photos of me on Twitter. Somehow her fans mobilized and posted pics that looked like me from the two months when I stripped (which by then was over twenty years earlier). They posted them in this "This you?" kind of way, suggesting that I was in no position to offer an opinion as a grown woman to another grown woman. I had never before felt the wrath of the internet like that. Not only was it humiliating, it was just so unnecessary. I even found myself tweeting back at the trolls, urging them to actually *listen* to what I was saying in the clip. But everyone knows that feeding the trolls only makes them come back hungrier— I just hated what was happening and didn't know how to handle it. I was annoyed that I even felt like I had to respond to them, especially when I wasn't really that active on social media to begin with. I wanted no part of that version of the internet, where you fall victim to kids playing in the shadows of the dark web trying to expose people and then you're out there yelling back at them. It's just not me and it's not my personality. I was pushing forty, feeling like *get me off this ride, I'm not going to look unhinged.* Good thing I have some good friends in high places, because everything embarrassing was basically wiped from the internet pretty quickly, but that didn't calm the embarrassment that I felt from within. Suddenly, being a daytime talk show host didn't seem like the best idea after all.

When I first started as a guest cohost on *The Talk* in the fall of 2017, it seemed like a lot of fun. You show up a few times, you offer a few thoughts, and then it's over. After Aisha Tyler left the show, the rotating chair of guest hosts was going to culminate in one receiving a permanent position—and I was in the running for that position. I wanted the job, but I don't think I really understood what the job was until I was permanently in that seat. Once I found out that I was going to be the new cohost, I was so excited, but very quickly reality set in. Now I had to expose myself to the public...every day. That idea alone seemed scary, but I couldn't even fathom just how scary it was until I saw those pictures of myself online.

Here's the thing about my inner peace: I worked so hard to get it. For so long I was without it, and when you're in the thick of the music industry, you don't even know what the hell it even is. I knew firsthand just how bad it can get in your own mind, and how that can completely destroy you. A sense of peace was essential to me, and once I finally found it, it became so precious. It was my sacred place, and I wasn't going to let anything rattle it, not even a talk show, and especially not someone else's fan base.

"I'm gonna quit," I told my stylist Lexy. "That's what I'm gonna do." One of the only demands that I had when joining *The Talk* was that I had to bring my own stylist plus hair and makeup with me. Eventually, though, I did use an in-house stylist who was also great. I needed someone that I could trust. Also, if it wasn't for Lexy, who was my long-time friend and knew me so well, then I might have quit the show altogether after my doxing. I felt the anxiety building as I told her that I was never heading back on set again. "You're not quitting," she said. "No, but I am," I said back to her. "I'm not going back to work." She told me to just breathe and understand that this will all blow over. "You're fine," she added. "It'll be over soon." It felt so permanent in the moment. I wasn't used to being a part of the public in that way, where my words had the potential to cause chaos. My music was a different story; that was my art and I understood that it's subject to criticism. But dragging me for a comment I'd made on national television, one that was taken out of context? Yeah, no thanks. Plus, it was like one of those instances where you ask yourself just how many times you have to be resilient and how many times good things have to become so fucked up?

Eventually, though, Lexy calmed me down and talked me off the ledge, and I showed back up to work. Thankfully, the internet has a very short attention span, so they forgot about my comment as fast as they were on it. That was a learning lesson for me—not to stop talking, but to recognize that when you talk, everyone might be listening. I was always conscientious about what I put out into the world, especially in a public forum. But it was a different world on *The Talk*, where the whole point was to share your opinion. Sometimes the majority of those listening will agree with you, and sometimes they won't. And while Nicki's fan base was just a small part of the equation (and an even smaller part of the world), they were destructive enough to briefly mess with me mentally. It was horrible, but I moved past it and kept going. You kind of have to in order to experience new things. I had to check myself and say, "You know what? You're still alive, and none of this really matters." What did matter was how I had to adjust to yet another new position in my life and career. Trying new things can lead to shit like that sometimes. I was definitely taking baby steps when I walked onto the set of *The Talk*, in more ways than one.

Vulnerability was never my thing. I never really wanted anyone to know that much about what I was feeling, outside of maybe the people closest to me and my mental health professionals. Even in my music, I'd go there with my emotions, but I never really *went* there. I had set my own limits to just how extensively I would emote in front of people, even when I was rapping. *The Talk* is what really dismantled that mind set, mainly because that was *the job*. I couldn't exactly show up on set, where everyone was seemingly baring their soul, and be the only one who was guarded. Another (major) thing was that I was terrified of public speaking. It was one of my biggest fears. Get me on the mic to rap and I'm fine. Put me on a movie set and I can recite my lines with no problem. But have me there on set, talking to the people while everyone else is silent, and I freeze up. I had to learn how to shake that off pretty quickly. I also had to learn how to be physically uncomfortable. We had a "makeup-free" episode within the first few months of filming, where we all had to be on camera with no makeup on our faces. That took me *way* out of my comfort zone, since I hadn't been barefaced in front of a camera since my Ruff Ryder days, and even then I at least had on some concealer. Since my cohosts were also not wearing any makeup, there was solidarity in that moment and I felt empowered to do it too. It was like a community was forming, one I had never experienced before, in front of a live studio audience. So gradually, I opened up more for the cameras, for the audience, and for my cohosts.

Eventually, though, I started to realize something: *everyone else* on the show was acting, just as I was trying so hard *not* to act. Since I came from a place where showing your emotions meant you were sharing something real, it hadn't really clicked that you can be publicly emotive while still totally playing a role. It knocked me right over once I came to that conclusion. It started when Julie Chen Moonves's husband, Les, had an alleged #MeToo situation and the rest of the girls basically shunned her for it. Les was the former chief executive at our network, CBS, and it was no secret how Julie was judged for that seeming nepotism. But to me, something like what happened with her husband and his alleged sexual misconduct had no bearing on how we were supposed to feel about Julie. Plus, everyone seemed to be so friendly with each other. So I texted her and checked on her. I felt like it was the right thing to do. My cohosts were a little shocked by that, because the whole setup on the show was kind of like *The Hunger Games*, where if you got knocked off your seat then so be it. Within a few months of Julie's husband's scandal, she made the decision to leave, and afterward everyone acted like she was never a part of it. It was like *that*.

Much like when I first entered the arena as a rapper, I'd thought all of the girls were friends, and once again I was proven wrong. Things started to get pettier on and off camera. We were having a conversation off camera one time about a very specific (and touchy) subject—one that I was really passionate about but my cohost wasn't. She kept on disagreeing with me, but I could tell she wasn't informed at all about what she was talking about. So I doubled down—like I said, I was passionate about it. By the time the cameras started rolling and the topic was brought up, she spoke first—using *my* opinion and not hers, as if these were her own thoughts and feelings. I was like, "Oh wow, okay, so this is what we're doing now?" So I jumped back in like, "That's a great standpoint, I agree with you," and I started adding more to what she had said (mainly because she had nothing else to say). That's also when I realized that what was coming out of my cohosts' mouths wasn't always their true feelings or opinions.

It was so weirdly toxic, and people kept coming and going. There was no way those musical chairs didn't look crazy to the rest of the world, and I think the network realized it. Something had to be done to manufacture some cast morale. The crew had asked us to stage a dinner with each other and then invited the paparazzi to show, so that everyone thought we were all friends and went out to dinner together frequently. That happened one time and one time only. Then we were all sent to Las Vegas to watch Marie Osmond and her brother Donny perform at their show. More paparazzi came. And despite that, Marie left the show a few months after that. By the time I reached the halfway mark of my time on *The Talk*, nearly half of the cast that I had started with had already left the show. I don't want to put it all onto my cohosts, because I started to fit into that culture as well. It's like you become a Mean Girl when you're surrounded by them. I had to have a reality check with myself yet again to cut the shit and get back to the person that I am. Deep down, I wanted to leave the show, but I didn't want to leave the opportunity.

My saving grace, ironically, was when the pandemic hit and I was isolated from everyone there since I was in London. Even then, you could still feel the unraveling from our laptop screens. My cohosts wanted to stage a coup to have our producer fired, and so they pulled me to the side to have me speak with the team. "You're younger and newer," they said. "They'll listen to you." While I understood some of the points they were making, for me it was the cattiness that had reached a boiling point. When I first arrived on *The Talk*, chaos came soon after. Aisha had left on her own terms, but so many of the cohosts were on that show for damn near a decade. So I replaced Aisha, then Julie left, then another cohost, then another. These seats starts turning over, and with each one came new personalities that had to assimilate to one another. While that producer eventually *did* get fired (not really for my cohosts' reasons, but seemingly also his poor handling of #BlackLivesMatter and the heightened racial injustices that started intensifying during the pandemic), the cohosts who were there the longest still felt like they needed someone new (i.e., *me*) to complain for them, since they weren't being heard. Again, I understood it, but it wasn't a position that I wanted to be in.

Being on Zoom during quarantine—and later in my own studio in London once things got a little safer—was the distance that kept me there longer. Being separated from the pack, yet still having the opportunity to speak my opinions, helped me feel comfortably removed from any interpersonal shit happening behind the scenes. Nothing had to be staged, and I didn't have to think about what everyone was *really* thinking. As the world started opening up, I realized that I had to make a decision, and I really didn't want to return to LA. For one, it was the first time in my relationship with Max that we were able to spend that much time together. Even once we were married, I was living in Atlanta for three months, then in Los Angeles, and basically commuting back and forth. I got to really know my husband and love him even more than I already had, and the idea of physically returning to *The Talk* was so upsetting to me. So I used it as my excuse to not return to *The Talk*. I cried during the last episode, and those tears were real. The show basically taught me that it was okay to do that on camera.

We had some important moments together, like when Julie Andrews came on the show and I cried my eyes out because it reminded me of my childhood watching her during Christmas in *The Sound of Music*. And even though there was some *acting* going on, I do consider some of the girls my friends. I loved them individually, and all for different reasons. Sheryl was cool, Carrie Ann was cool, and Sharon Osbourne (who I affectionately called Mrs. O) was cool. When she eventually left the show, I felt for her, because we were urged to be opinionated and Mrs. O loved to express her opinions. But sometimes those opinions can backfire. It brought me back to that first week on the job, when my opinions got me into trouble.

The Talk even gave me a space to discuss hip-hop and whatever else was on my mind. I had never been in a position where that wasn't just reserved for music. Not to mention I had a place to really express my feelings at a time when the world was experiencing yet another wave of racial injustice. Even though the show was hard to maneuver and personalities clashed, it was what I needed when I had it.

I'd never had a podium like the one that I had on *The Talk*, and now I know that when I get it again, I will know how to use it.

19

QUEENS

There's a reason why I never really wanted to be in a girl group, and those feelings were totally reinforced when I became a "Nasty Bitch."

When the opportunity came for me to film *Queens*, it seemed like a good idea. I had just left *The Talk* the year before, and I was ready to get back into acting, or at least do something that didn't involve a talk show. I was back into making music a little bit, too. I even collaborated with Doja Cat on her song "Tonight" and got another Grammy nomination. Max and I were actively trying to get pregnant, but we hadn't yet, and then this opportunity for *Queens* came to me. The plotline was cool—an all-girl rap group reunites after twenty-something years and tries to make it big again when their most popular single is sampled by a newer artist. Swizz was involved as the show's composer, and I was starring alongside other seasoned artists like Brandy and

Naturi Naughton. Pepi Sonuga was also a recording artist and she was really talented. I have to give it up to Nadine Velazquez, though, because even though she wasn't an artist she killed her role on that show from Day One. *Queens* had an excellent concept behind it, but by the time it reached execution, everything started unraveling.

I knew immediately after we shot the pilot that I would not be returning for a second season.

The storyline of my character on the show, Brianna—aka Professor Sex—had a lot of overlap in my own life. She was a wife and the mother of five children. Meanwhile, I was a wife with four bonus kids, trying to have a child (which would then make five). She was struggling with her identity, portraying her rap self again while still living out her day-to-day role as a wife and mother. That was also something that resonated with me, since I understood trying to balance being a homemaker with being a celebrity. It all clicked for me. Brianna had a very complicated storyline, to say the least. First she finds out that her husband is cheating. Then he gets diagnosed with brain cancer, as Brianna is still trying to figure out whether or not she can forgive him and move forward in their marriage—all while trying to reassemble this girl group. Her husband ends up dying, and she finds out at the funeral that his mistress was pregnant. Then Brianna gets shot. Like, what? We all had these very strangely detailed storylines that were full of dramatic moments. Thankfully, I couldn't relate to *any* of that other stuff in my character's storyline, but I did appreciate that Brianna had some layers beyond just being known as "Professor Sex." That and the fact that I got to rap on the show too. In one scene, Brandy's character and my character even battle, and we all did a cypher. That was great, especially since it was a cypher of all women, which is the exact opposite of what I was used to seeing in real life as a rapper.

The writers of the show tried their best to make it as realistic as possible, and there was a clear attention to detail for the artists and the artistry, and it reflected actual things that could have happened in the music industry. While we weren't allowed to change *anything* in the script, the writers did share things with us. For example, when my character battled Brandy's, the head writer told me that there was no way that I was going to lose that battle either way. I guess it was because in their minds it wasn't Brandy's character, Xplicit Lyrics, battling Professor Sex; it was Brandy battling Eve. It was an ambitious show, maybe *too* ambitious for its own good, where it was trying to be too many things at once.

The thing about *Queens* was that from the start, nobody knew if it was going to be picked up for a second season. This was all a trial run, and it felt like nobody embraced leaning into that uncertainty to still make it a successful show. For me, I was still on that journey of peace, and after leaving *The Talk*, I absolutely did not want to enter into any toxic work environments again. Needless to say, *Queens* was not the peaceful place that I had hoped for. The dynamic amongst us girls was just totally off. Individually, I loved them dearly, but as a group, shit was always just hitting the fan. Sometimes people were friends, then they were enemies. There were arguments amongst each other, to the point where there was screaming, yelling, and crying—all of that. Sometimes I was thrown into the middle of it, and then other times I was watching like, "What the hell is actually happening?" People started just going at each other, and I was mostly just confused, reminding them all that none of this was real. Then at one point, when things were super intense, the girls were like, "Let's all pray together in one of our trailers," and I'm like, "What the fuck? No. Enough of this already." I tried to always remain neutral in the middle of the drama, and never really take sides, but it was just a lot of different emotions happening between us all at once. Basically, we started *acting* like we were an *actual* group, and I totally understand why. It was hard to break character when three quarters of the group were already recording artists. We recorded songs, made music videos, technically "performed" together...like I get it. It was easy to forget that we weren't all a group, but once I was wrapped up in the middle of the Nasty Bitches turned Queens, it felt real, and I wanted to "quit the band."

There was something else that was going on in my life while I was on set: I found out that I was pregnant. And I was terrified.

Swizz was actually one of the first people that I had to tell, because I was supposed to battle Trina in Miami for *Verzuz* right before we went to film *Queens*. Once I learned that I was pregnant, I told him I couldn't be a part of *Verzuz*. I was afraid to fly to Miami out of fear that I would lose the baby. Swizz didn't know that when I first turned him down. He said to me, "Why aren't you getting on that plane? I'll send you a jet!" I finally had to tell him, and he was like, "Say no more. We'll figure it out." He knew how long I'd wanted to be a mother and did what he had to do. So instead, Trina and I did our *Verzuz* battle remotely, like the artists did in the heart of the pandemic. Meanwhile, I was so worried about my baby that I was kind of afraid to rap! I didn't know if I could raise my voice or be near loud music, let alone get on an airplane to go do it. I eventually had to shake that fear after talking to my doctor, because I'd already signed up for *Queens*.

When I first read the show's script and agreed to be on

it, I wasn't yet pregnant, but still trying. By the time we shot the pilot and the show was greenlit, I was. My character, Brianna, was number one on the call sheet, which I appreciated and was grateful for, but that basically meant I had the most rigorous schedule with the most scenes. The shooting schedule in general for that show was out of control, but as a newly pregnant woman, I was just ill-equipped to handle it from the jump.

I pulled the head writer aside to have a talk like, "Look, I know you want to have me in all of these scenes and doing all of this stuff, but I just don't think I'm physically able to do it." I understood that people got pregnant all the time and still worked, so I wasn't looking for his sympathy, but I had hoped for a little understanding because his wife had just had a baby like two weeks before we started filming. Instead, I felt like I wasn't being heard. Tensions started running even higher because I didn't feel like I was given any grace as a pregnant woman when it came to the length of time I was on set. We ended up getting into a huge fight one night, because he wanted me to change up my wig for a scene, which would have had me on set until three o'clock in the morning. I had to finally say to him, "Would you do that to your wife?" He got upset and said, "You don't think I care about your well-being?" I simply replied, "No, you don't." As a producer on a show, I understand that you need to get the job done, but come on now. It was getting ridiculous. I even asked to be moved from number one on the call sheet, like "Bump me down then, if that's what needs to be done." It would be more of a symbolic gesture than anything, since being number one gave me a prominent storyline, but all of the storylines were intertwined anyway. It was just a lot. I wasn't alone, though, because everyone on set had a problem with *something*. I don't think anyone really felt like the show ran smoothly or had an all-around positive experience. But the girls and I were total professionals about it, and when we did our press run for the series, we handled it the way we were supposed to. We really looked like a girl group that was hiding their inner struggles while still smiling for the cameras.

In reality, though, my anxiety took over once I was pregnant. I had waited so long for it to finally happen that I didn't even know how to function once it did. I called my doctor constantly from the set. I even went to a doctor out there in Atlanta while we were filming just so that I could hear my baby's heartbeat. While I kept my poker face on set, I called Max every night crying, almost completely hysterical. I was just so worried that the stress of the show was going to lead to me losing my baby. I kept asking myself, "What if I lose this kid? What if my work jeopardizes this pregnancy?"

Max had to calm me down every time, if not for my sake, then for the baby's. There was a lot of internal shit going on with me emotionally that only made the experience feel even worse. I know that a lot of it was hormonal, but the environment didn't help at all. I reached my breaking point when a crew member caught COVID, and that's when I absolutely spiraled. We had all of these safety measures in place, but none were going to keep us completely safe. They shut the set down for the day, and then two crew members pulled me to the side and said, "Look, you were around this person for sixteen hours. We are only letting you know because you're pregnant." That was it. I couldn't stop screaming and crying. Naturi and Brandy had to pull me into a trailer to calm me down, because I kept shouting, "Fuck y'all! You don't give a fuck about anyone! I'm pregnant and you had me around this fucking person for sixteen fucking hours?" All I could imagine was catching COVID and hurting my baby, all because I wanted to film this fucking show where everyone was fighting and that I was already over. That was my last straw. The show broke my peace, and I wanted out.

Maybe *Queens* just happened at the wrong place and the wrong time in my life. I never imagined having to be a part of something so physically and emotionally draining while carrying my first child. Over the several months of filming, I became even more pregnant-looking, obviously, but the problem was that the show's scenes were all shot out of order. So there would be a scene where I looked fuller in my face and body due to my pregnancy, and then in others I'm back to my normal size. It looked kind of crazy, like my body was just fluctuating up and down, depending on the episode or even the scene. Everything about that *Queens* experience was just so chaotic, right down to how Brianna's storyline unfolded.

Since we still didn't know if we were getting picked up for season two—and because I had to go have my baby—they opted to shoot Brianna and put her in a coma in the hospital. That way, if we got picked up, we could have her survive. It was the show's way of giving me that opportunity to come back if I wanted to. I already knew that I wasn't returning to that show for a second season. And if I did, then it would be for like three episodes (*maybe* four, max) to finish off my character's storyline. Instead, they made Brianna appear dead halfway through the series, but then it turned out she actually just moved to the islands to take a break. In the end, she had no desire to return to the group and everything that went with it, but she left the door open just in case she did want to pop back in at some point. I related to the end of Brianna's storyline so much, because I too just wanted to run away to an island with my family after that whole experience.

My biggest takeaway from *Queens*, though, is that I will never again walk onto a television set without some sort of a credit beyond that of a working actor. I'd started on my own TV series where I both starred and was an executive producer, so returning to scripted television with no power felt like I was moving backwards. I saw how that affected the way in which we were treated, the way the storylines were created, and how decisions were being made for us. If I'm getting back on a television series now, then I'm executive producing it at the very least. Otherwise, no thank you.

I can't say that *Queens* was all bad, though. I loved being able to get back into rapping, wearing costumes and performing like I did when being a full-time rapper was my job. In a sense, it prepared me for what would inevitably be my return to the stage after I had my son. It was also rewarding to know that people really *did* like that show, regardless of what was going down behind the scenes. There are clips on social media that still treat our musical moments on the series like they happened in real life, and while in the moment I was fighting to keep everyone in reality, it's cool to see those clips in hindsight. I'll never forget how I was in New York City two years after the show was filmed, when a security guard stopped me at a UN event that I was hosting. She said to me, "You killed that battle with Brandy! When I saw that, I knew my girl Eve was gonna take it!" I smiled at her and thanked her. She reminded me that even though the situation might not have been the best, we all still made the most of it. And I got to return to form for a bit as my rapper self while I was preparing to be a mom.

Don't get it confused, though: Brandy's got some bars too.

20

BORN TO BE WILDE

I told them all it was appendicitis.

It was 2006, and I was still filming my *Eve* TV series, when I found out that I was pregnant. It was called a tubal pregnancy, where the embryonic sac ruptured in my one fallopian tube. It's also known as an ectopic pregnancy. I had to have emergency surgery and stop filming the show for two weeks. I don't know why I lied to everyone on set and said that my appendix had ruptured, really. Maybe because I was lying to myself. If I faced losing my baby, then I didn't know if two weeks would be enough emotional healing time. In the end, it was barely enough healing time for me physically, before I was right back to work on set. I had lost so much weight after the surgery, and my body was so frail. I still had to walk red carpets during that time, and when I look back at pictures, I can see how skinny I was. Too skinny. And too much in denial. But it's like I've said before, sometimes I did whatever it took to show up and get the job done...even if it was to my own detriment.

For years, I never grieved losing my first baby. I didn't know how to, but I eventually learned. I had to speak to that baby and acknowledge their existence. I had to forgive myself and know that what had happened wasn't my fault, that I deserved to be a mother, and that I was ready to bring a baby into this world down here.

And his name would be Wilde Wolf.

For a long time after that first miscarriage, I didn't really try to get pregnant, and I didn't even think about trying until I met Max. I never thought it would be that difficult, because I had already gotten pregnant in the past, and even though it wasn't successful, it still happened. Max and I did try even before our wedding—once things had gotten really serious—but it didn't happen. I chalked it up to traveling too much, going back and forth to see him, being stressed from touring, whatever. Reproductive issues were the last thing on my mind. After Max and I were married for a while, we had begun to wonder why I wasn't getting pregnant. We really wanted one more child to complete this family unit that we had built together. Then my bonus kids started getting older, and Max's sisters started getting pregnant. I still wasn't. It got to a point where I had just resolved that maybe it wasn't in the cards for us. Maybe I was going to have my four bonus kids and that would be it. I was still happy with that, though reality would hit me in waves. When we would be at family parties and Max's relatives would be there with their kids, I started to feel that void. I would go home crying, because I felt so left out of something that I really and truly wanted. At the same time, it felt like my body was betraying me and the doctors just couldn't figure out why.

Back when I had first gotten pregnant, in 2006, my doctor never told me that one of my fallopian tubes was narrowed—the one that caused the rupture—and that it was covered in endometriosis. I could have had a procedure called a tubal ligation that would have fixed it, but none of that was ever told to me. Back then, even discussing things like endometriosis was completely taboo. People barely knew what it even was. And that kind of procedure is better to have done when you're younger, since it gets harder as you get older. Again, no one told me any of this. I know now that I also had fibroids, which so many people do—but I had *a lot* of them. At first when I went to different doctors, they said they only saw like three fibroids, maybe four, which they said was fine. Pregnancy shouldn't be difficult. It was recommended that I complete a round of IVF, which I didn't want to do at all. The whole process seemed so daunting, but I still went with it. That first round was torture, where my hormones were out of control and my natural menstrual cycle was completely shut down. Plus, I still didn't get pregnant. I had to get all of these injections to jump-start my cycle again, and I left that experience in a state of fear and trauma. I went from doctor to doctor, but I wasn't getting the answers or attention that I needed. I finally found a female doctor who figured it all out. Her name is Dr. Thais Aliabadi, and she was the first doctor who ever listened to me.

As a woman, as a *Black* woman, reproductive health is a roller coaster ride with seemingly no safety bar. For my whole life, I was made to feel that my periods should be painful, and that was the price you pay as a woman. That couldn't be further from the truth. Your periods *shouldn't* hurt that badly and you *shouldn't* be ignored when they do. I learned all that from Dr. Aliabadi. I'd had so many exams with other doctors who kept telling me that I only had like three fibroids, but she found fourteen of them, with one big one attached to my uterine wall. There was no way that I was getting pregnant with that sitting in there. I finally had an ablation procedure to remove them all. By the time I had my next period after the ablation, I started to cry because I *wasn't* in pain. I had never felt that way before. It was like my uterus was brand-new, ready for my baby to arrive. I was ready to go back out there and try to get pregnant.

I had two more rounds of IVF after that first traumatic one. During the second round, I had one embryo. It was tested and they found that it was a mosaic embryo, where the baby might be born with potential genetic issues. That didn't matter to me, though, and so we froze it and opted to continue going back-to-back with IVF rounds for another embryo just in case. By the next round, we had a perfect embryo. The next step was to have it implanted inside me. So we scheduled my implantation day, where I would go in, and they would thaw the embryo out and put it inside me to see if the magic would happen.

I went to get my hair blown out that morning. I wanted to look nice for my baby. I was dressed in all orange for my Sacral Chakra, right where my baby was heading. I wore a pretty dress with orange flowers, along with orange sandals and an orange bag. While I was getting my hair blown dry, I received a phone call. "Hello, Mrs. Cooper, we have a bit of an issue. It seems as though your embryo has dissolved." I was in total shock. I hadn't even known that could happen. I immediately started crying. "What do you mean?" I said. "How could the embryo just dissolve like that?" Apparently it could. The doctor said, "Since you're coming in, would you like us to thaw that second embryo?" It was the mosaic one. Through tears, I said, "Yes, of course." I went through with my implantation as planned, only with the mosaic embryo.

That mosaic embryo that made it was my baby Wilde.

He was my soul baby, and he was meant to be here. Before I even knew I was having a boy, I kept referring to my baby as a "he." The doctors kept asking me why I kept calling the baby a "he," and I said, "I don't know, I just think I'm having a boy." I also knew that he was going to be totally fine when he was born. I meditated a lot, I did acupuncture, I tried to make my body as peaceful as possible for this fertilization to work, and when it did, I just knew he was going to be okay. And he was. After the chaos of *Queens*, I headed back home to continue my pregnancy and bring myself back to that peaceful place for my baby to enter the world.

On February 1, 2022, Wilde Wolf Fife Alexander Somers Cooper was born. I remember when I first posted about my baby on Instagram, someone said, "I know she wanted that baby badly. She used all of her names."

We had so many names for Wilde at first, and so many different signs that led us to those names. Our top two were Jedi and Orion. I used to play David Bowie's "Starman" while I was pregnant, because he was my little Starman. I thought of the name Orion since it's a constellation, and so I called Max while he was away in Atlanta to ask him what he thought of it. A few hours later, he was in a studio with Dallas Austin and saw the name "Orion" written on the wall of his studio. Then I came up with Jedi, which I know sounds crazy, but it sounded so cool to me. I was still filming *Queens* at the time, and so I went downstairs in the complex that I was staying in to get some food and a giant cutout of a Jedi was right there. We didn't use either of those names, but it was crazy how many times they popped up. No matter what, though, I was going to call him Wolf, but not as his first name, because like every kid in England is named Wolf. But the word *Lupus* from the Lupus constellation is Latin for "Wolf," so my little Starman still got that name. As for Wilde? I named him that so that he could have a free spirit. I never felt like I had a free-spirited childhood or the luxury of being just a kid, where I could be wild and happy and carefree. I wanted him to have that name so that he could always take that freedom with him wherever he went in life.

After Wilde was born, I fully embraced being his mother. Every moment he was fed, every moment he cried, everything—I took it all in. But the thing they don't prepare you for is the identity shift that happens, especially when you have a baby at the age of forty-three like I did. That means I spent forty-three whole years as myself, and now I was someone's mother. And while it's the most rewarding thing in the entire world, it's a total shift in consciousness. I was definitely trying to figure out what that all meant. Who was I now? I didn't know. I started to imagine myself as two separate people, in a way. It's that superhero uniform that I wear onstage, but I don't take it home anymore. It's like that expression, "Don't take the office home with you." I'm still a superhero, but the word has multiple meanings for me now.

I still remember the night I had my first performance after having Wilde. It was a small corporate event, which for me was the perfect performance to come back with because it was "low-risk." People would be there eating, drinking; I wasn't totally the main focus. There were only like three hundred people at the event, which is smaller than most crowds that I've played for. But I remember I came home later that night at around eleven or so, and Wilde woke up once I got home. I was still fully glammed up in a Valentino suit, with my hair and makeup done. I went and made him a bottle and I picked him up from his crib and sat in a chair in my full glam, and rocked him back to sleep in my arms with his bottle. There was something about that moment—I said to myself, "Oh, this is fucking *cool.*" I know it seems so small, but it really was the moment where it all clicked for me, like, "I can do this. I can still be Eve and still be Wilde's mom, and that's okay."

As an older mom, though, the most important thing to me is being there for every moment in my son's young life. That means sacrificing extended work events if he can't come with me or turning down opportunities if it means I'll be away from him for too long. I don't want to miss anything. I don't want to look back and regret choosing a job over spending his life with him. After all that time I spent waiting for Wilde, I'm not taking one second with him for granted. I have to be the most available for him and only him. Period.

I look at my Wilde sometimes, and I just say to him, "Thank you for choosing me." There were times in my life when I didn't feel safe in this world, and I am just so thankful that I can be his safe place—the one place where he can go and cry when he needs me. I didn't always have that, but I am so happy that he always will.

EPILOGUE

A MOTHER ON THE MIC

I was standing on the side of the stage at the Las Vegas Festival Grounds, there for the Lovers and Friends fest, ready to perform, and for the first time in my career, I felt uncertain. I had just given birth to Wilde a little over a year before, and I wasn't totally comfortable in my post-baby body. I didn't feel the same and I definitely didn't look the same. That was going to be the first time that an audience of that size would see me onstage since I gave birth. It was also my first festival in nearly a decade. I needed everything to be *perfect* for this performance—from my outfit, to my hair, my makeup, my dancers, my DJ, my graphics. All of it. If I was going back "outside," as they say, then I had to do it right. Still, I was nervous. I didn't really know my dancers that well, I was surviving on no sleep plus jet lag after an eleven-hour flight, and there I was, about to perform alongside my peers. I knew it was now or never, though.

As the music started playing, I felt plugged in. That's when I transformed again, going back into my proverbial phone booth to put on my superhero cape and jump back out. As soon as I hit that stage, I was back in rare form. I was back to me, Eve, but a remixed version of me. A different one, a happier one. I had my mother and my son with me this time. It was a whole new experience. This was the first day of the rest of my career, and there was a feeling of completeness to it all.

When I opened up my set, I chose to perform "Ruff Ryders' Anthem" in memory of DMX. Right after he died, I remember feeling guilty that I didn't get to attend his actual funeral for a more personal farewell. He later came to me in a dream instead, where I got to see him at peace, and I got to say goodbye to him. So hitting a stage for the first time again, he was one of the first people on my mind, and so I had to honor him. As I moved through my catalog during my set, I saw my fans in the audience reciting my lyrics word for word. Sometimes you forget the impact that you can have on people's lives until they're right there in front of you, chanting the lyrics that you once wrote by hand on the pages of a notepad in an SUV in Harlem or a dark studio in Los Angeles. The truth is that I never got to stop and think about any of that until I hit pause on my career for a little bit. So coming back out there, I was able to really take it all in for the first time ever. And it felt amazing.

As I sit and think about my journey, both with the Ruff Ryders and on my own, through all the twists and turns that my life has taken me, I feel an overwhelming sense of gratitude. I'm a different person from that young girl who was rapping like her life depended on it. I'm a wife now, a mother to a beautiful son and four amazing bonus kids.

I'm a philanthropist, whose proudest moment was becoming a Goodwill Ambassador for Malaika, an organization that builds schools and provides resources for children in the DR Congo. I'm an actor, with countless movie and TV roles that I'm proud of, and more to come. But most of all, I'm still that girl from Philly who can rap her ass off. The best part about it all is that now I've finally learned that I can be all of those women when I want to be. The superhero cape doesn't actually leave me—it just switches.

So much has changed since I first entered the hip-hop world. Women don't exactly have it easier, yet they can do some of the things that took me years to realize I could do. When I was pregnant, I was inspired by artists like Cardi B, who understood way earlier than I did that you can be a mother and still be a rapper. I came from an era when women weren't even sure if they were allowed to be mothers. Lauryn Hill talks about that in "To Zion," where people in the music industry brought up her career once she learned she was pregnant. Having kids wasn't something that we were encouraged to do. A lot of rappers are out there as mothers now, though, which is cool to see, since there were hardly any when I first arrived. I'd be lying if I said that I'd do it all over again differently, because maybe the outcome would have been different. Everything happened exactly when it was supposed to.

Before we reached Las Vegas for Lovers and Friends, we stopped in Los Angeles, and I remember looking out the windows of my hotel at the Hollywood Hills. These were the same hills where I used to go to house parties, drink with no restraint, yet now I was there with my child. Life is crazy like that. It reminds you that everything can change, and that change can be beautiful. As a kid, I might have thought that I was cursed with the name Eve, but now I finally know who Eve is. I know that in so many ways I changed the course of hip-hop, especially for women. I showed these girls how to rap with bars first and body second. How to be the only woman in your crew, but still be the most highly respected member. How to pivot—whether it's into fashion, film, TV, whatever. How to navigate through the treacherous waters of the music industry, and figure it all out along the way. And how to do it all with grace and as much inner peace as possible.

This isn't some retirement letter, though. There's too much left to do. But while I'll continue to work (whatever that means and in whatever form), my desire for the hustle that nearly broke me is gone. I just don't have the energy to return to that place, and I pray that I never will. I still love working hard, though, I still love creating, and I still love performing. But I do believe in that "soft" life, especially now that I'm living in it.

The *ride* isn't as *rough* anymore, and I'm enjoying every minute of it.

★ ★ ★ ★ ★

ACKNOWLEDGMENTS

EVE

This book would not be possible without the following people.

To my co-writer, Kathy Iandoli: thank you for helping me through this process and making it so fun. It came together perfectly.

To all of my fans everywhere: thank you for riding with me all these years, and to Philly, the best city ever!

To my family: Mom (you are the best), my dad, Ron; my brother, Farrod; my cousin Takeya; Uncle Jimmy; Uncle Johnnie; my dad, Jerry Jeffers and my Jeffers family; Grandma; Aunt Penny; Aunt Bernice; and all of my family not named. I love you all. To my aunt Karen, my Grandpop, and my uncle Jeffrey, may they rest.

To my hubby, Maximillion, for the literal adventures and support. I love you. Wilde, my little Star Man, for making me whole. Lotus, Jagger, Cash and Mini: it has been such a joy watching you grow. I am so grateful to have you all in my life. Best bonus kids ever. To all of my Cooper family and extended family, thank you. And to my dog, Hendrix…yes, my dog.

To all my friends who have seen me in and through shit:

Erin aka "elefty;" Mitch and Matt Moinian, for giving me a place to stay when I really needed it over the years. Lexy Rose, Lauren Imparato, Angela Stevens, Ernesto Casillas, Taryn Charles, Noella Coursaris Musunka and the staff at Malaika DRC, thank you.

To Peter Joseph, Eden Railsback, Emer Flounders and everyone at Hanover Square Press/HarperCollins who made this book possible. To Robert Guinsler and Sterling Lord Literistic, Wayne Russell, Billy Clark, Pippa Wealthall and my team at Massive Management. Thank you all for your excitement and hard work on this book.

A big thank-you to Waah, Dee, Chivon Dean, Swizz Beats and all of my Ruff Ryders family (RIP DMX and Icepick).

To everyone mentioned in this book: Thank you for being a part of my story in whatever way.

KATHY IANDOLI

To Eve, thank you for choosing me to ride shotgun on this journey. Congrats, Scorpio, you're stuck with me now. Love, Pisces.

To my mom up in heaven, who was always tied for first with me as Eve's Number One Fan: I see what you did here. Thank you.

To Robert Guinsler, Sterling Lord Literistic, Peter Joseph, Eden Railsback, Emer Flounders and everyone at Hanover Square Press/HarperCollins. Thank you.

To my dogter, Indie, who runs into the room whenever she hears Eve's voice because she loves the sound of it. I feel you, doggy.

To all of my family and friends who have supported me on this journey. You know who you are. Thank you, and I love you all.